What Works in Work-First Welfare

What Works in Work-First Welfare

Designing and Managing Employment Programs in New York City

Andrew R. Feldman

2011

W.E. Upjohn Institute for Employment Research
Kalamazoo, Michigan

Library of Congress Cataloging-in-Publication Data

Feldman, Andrew R.
  What works in work-first welfare : designing and managing employment programs in New York City / Andrew R. Feldman.
     p. cm.
  Includes bibliographical references and index.
  ISBN-13: 978-0-88099-375-3 (pbk. : alk. paper)
  ISBN-10: 0-88099-375-8 (pbk. : alk. paper)
  ISBN-13: 978-0-88099-376-0 (hardcover : alk. paper)
  ISBN-10: 0-88099-376-6 (hardcover : alk. paper)
   1. Manpower policy—New York (State)—New York. 2. New York (N.Y.)—Social policy. 3. Public welfare—New York (State)—New York. 4. Employees—Recruiting—New York (State)—New York. 5. Leadership—New York (State)—New York. 6. Personnel management—New York (State)—New York. 7. Local officials and employees I. Title.
  HD5726.N5F45 2011
  362.5'84097471—dc22
                                    2010049641

© 2011
W.E. Upjohn Institute for Employment Research
300 S. Westnedge Avenue
Kalamazoo, Michigan 49007-4686

The facts presented in this study and the observations and viewpoints expressed are the sole responsibility of the author. They do not necessarily represent positions of the W.E. Upjohn Institute for Employment Research.

Cover design by Alcorn Publication Design.
Index prepared by Diane Worden.
Printed in the United States of America.
Printed on recycled paper.

Library
University of Texas
at San Antonio

To my parents, Elizabeth and Jerry,
for their love, support, and encouragement.

Contents

Acknowledgments	xiii
Foreword	xv

1	**Introduction**	1
	TANF and Other U.S. Employment and Training Programs	3
	The Need for Better Welfare-to-Work Practices	4
2	**Welfare to Work in New York City**	19
	Key Features	19
	What Employment Programs Do: An Overview	23

Part 1: Shared Strategic Elements among Work-First Employment Programs

3	**Creating a Spirit of Partnership**	33
	Rationale	34
	Techniques	36
	Variation in Approaches	39
4	**Getting Participants Job Ready**	43
	Rationale	44
	Techniques	46
	Variation in Approaches	49
5	**Making Good Job Matches**	51
	Rationale	52
	Techniques	53
	Variation in Approaches	56
6	**Promoting Employment Retention**	61
	Rationale	61
	Techniques	62
	Variation in Approaches	64

Part 2: Differences in Organizational Practices among Work-First Employment Programs

7 Different Practices among Programs   69
    Quick Placement versus Case Management   69
    Short-Term Job Training versus Immediate Job Search   77
    The Employability of Hard-to-Serve Individuals   82
    Sanctioning Participants for Noncompliance   85

8 Different Practices among Program Types   89
    Nonprofit versus For-Profit   89
    Compensation: Full versus Partial Performance-Based Pay   92
    Program Size   95
    Faith-Based versus Secular   98

Part 3: Explaining Performance Differences among Work-First Employment Programs

9 What Works within Work-First?   105
    Factors That Affect Performance   106
    Factors That Do Not Drive Performance   112
    Results by Gender   114
    The Effects of Adopting Better Practices   115

10 Nonprofits and For-Profits: A Closer Look   119
    The Dispersion of Practices and Results by Organizational Form   119
    Insights into the Practice of Creaming the Caseload   124

11 The Role of Management and Leadership   129
    How Management Matters: An Overview of the Literature   129
    Looking across Programs   131
    Looking at Programs with Similar Strategies   134
    The Importance of an Effective Strategy   137

12 Why Programs Choose Suboptimal Practices   139
    Imperfect Information   139
    Maximizing Alternative Definitions of Performance   140
    Competency Traps   141
    Identity Traps   142
    The Need for Innovation   143

Appendix A: Methodology 145

Appendix B: Using Guided Job Search 153

Appendix C: Chapter 9 Regression Results 157

References 165

The Author 171

Index 173

About the Institute 183

Figures

1.1	Common Elements of Work-First Programs' Service Strategies	8
2.1	Performance Payments for Employment Programs (per participant)	20
2.2	Outcomes for Individuals Assigned to Employment Programs	26
2.3	Outcomes for Active Program Participants	27
5.1	Commitment to Job Matching: An Example of Two Programs	57
7.1	Median Number of Days between Program Entry and Job Start Date, among Those Who Become Employed	70
7.2	Two Models of Moving to Self-Sufficiency	76
7.3	Percentage of Participants That Receive Training Vouchers	78
7.4	Deassignment Rates among Participants	83
7.5	Sanctioning Rates among Participants Who Are Not Deassigned	85
8.1	Organizational Practices among Nonprofit and For-Profit Programs	92
8.2	Organizational Practices among EarnFair Programs and Other Programs	94
8.3	Number of Participants per Program (average size of group arriving every two weeks)	96
8.4	Organizational Practices among Programs of Different Sizes	97
8.5	Organizational Practices among Faith-Based and Non-Faith-Based Programs	100

9.1	Performance of For-Profit and Nonprofit Programs	107
9.2	Average Number of Placement and Retention Milestones Achieved per 100 Participants	108
10.1	Placement Rates for For-Profit and Nonprofit Programs	122
10.2	Six-Month Caseload Employment Rates for For-Profit and Nonprofit Programs	122
10.3	Organizational Practices among For-Profit and Nonprofit Programs for Long-Term Custodial Welfare Recipients	127
10.4	Employment Outcomes among For-Profit and Nonprofit Programs for Long-Term Custodial Welfare Recipients	127
11.1	Six-Month Caseload Employment Rates	133
11.2	Six-Month Caseload Employment Rates: Results for Programs with Slow Placement Speeds and/or That Encourage Job Training	138
A.1	Multilevel Model of Participant Outcomes	148
B.1	Guided Job Search as a Primary Job-Matching Tool	156

Tables

2.1	Employment Services and Placement (ESP) Programs	21
A.1	Program Characteristics	149
A.2	Participant Characteristics (%)	150
C.1	Participant Outcomes (%)	158
C.2	The Effects of Participant Characteristics, Economic Environment, and Organizational Characteristics on Performance, Measured as Job Placement for Custodial Participants	159
C.3	The Effects of Participant Characteristics, Economic Environment, and Organizational Characteristics on Performance, Measured as Job Placement with a High Wage for Placed Custodial Participants	161
C.4	The Effects of Participant Characteristics, Economic Environment, and Organizational Characteristics on Performance, Measured as Three-Month Employment Retention for Placed Custodial Participants	162

C.5	The Effects of Participant Characteristics, Economic Environment, and Organizational Characteristics on Performance, Measured as Six-Month Employment Retention for Placed Custodial Participants	163
C.6	The Effects of Participant Characteristics, Economic Environment, and Organizational Characteristics on Performance, Measured as Placed in a Job and Still Working at Any Job Six Months Later for Custodial Participants	164

Acknowledgments

The idea for this book came from Bryna Sanger of the Milano New School for Management and Urban Policy, whom I contacted after reading her book *The Welfare Marketplace*. After explaining my research interest in the intersection of poverty policy and public management, she suggested that I focus on performance issues—in particular, why some welfare-to-work programs are more effective than others. She also suggested that I contact New York City's welfare department (the Human Resources Administration or HRA), which was using random assignment to place welfare recipients into employment programs, creating a natural experiment that had not yet been carefully studied. Both were terrifically valuable suggestions. My research would not have progressed, moreover, without Swati Desai, HRA's Executive Deputy Commissioner at the time (now a professor at Columbia University), who wanted to shed new light on program performance and secured HRA authorization for me to study New York City's programs. Assistant Deputy Commissioner Lisa Garabedian also provided valuable help in many ways, from setting up my program visits to helping me understand the structure of HRA's administrative data.

This book has benefited enormously from the comments and suggestions of others. First and foremost are my colleagues at the Kennedy School of Government at Harvard University. Mary Jo Bane provided guidance and feedback throughout the research process, including key suggestions that shaped this study. She has been an important mentor to me. Jeff Liebman gave very useful feedback in terms of both methodology and presentation. And David Ellwood helped me think through the implications of my findings. At Harvard University, the Inequality and Social Policy Program (funded by the National Science Foundation) and the Malcolm Wiener Center for Social Policy provided financial support for this research.

My thanks go as well to Larry Mead of New York University who helped me formulate the study's design and gave me feedback on the results. His methodological work on performance analysis is a basis for this study. Bruce Ross-Larson helped me turn a more academic-oriented piece of research into a book for publication. A special thanks to Kevin Hollenbeck at the Upjohn Institute and three anonymous readers who provided extremely useful suggestions on the book's first draft. Carolyn Heinrich and her colleagues at the La Follette School of Public Policy at the University of Wisconsin also provided insightful comments on my research at a presentation there in early 2010. The book was copyedited by Bob Wathen, whose careful and thoughtful editing improved the manuscript significantly. Rich Wyrwa at the Upjohn Institute helped shepherd the book to publication.

My sincere thanks also go to the leaders of the 26 employment programs in New York City that are the focus of this volume. Their openness to having a researcher observe their programs and interview them and their staffs was critical to this research.

Finally, I would also like to acknowledge two scholars who have played important roles in my life and who therefore influenced this volume. Bob Behn at the Kennedy School inspired me, during graduate school, to add public management as one of my main research interests. His guidance and insights over the years have been invaluable. And Rob Hollister of Swarthmore College inspired me, in college, to become a poverty researcher. Since then Rob has been an important guiding influence to me, with his commitment to rigorous research, his sense of humor, and his generous spirit.

Foreword

In October 2004, Andy Feldman began doing the fieldwork for this book in the welfare-to-work programs of New York City. The welfare system in New York City, as in the nation as a whole, was in the midst of a massive transformation. The 1996 federal welfare reform legislation had promised to "end welfare as we know it," and in many ways it had succeeded. Nationally, welfare rolls fell by two-thirds between 1994, their peak, and 2005. In New York City, the number of people receiving welfare fell from 1.1 million in the spring of 1995 to 420,000 in March 2005 when Andy was finishing his fieldwork. Caseloads have continued to fall, even in the midst of the serious recession of 2007–2009. Nationally, the Temporary Assistance to Needy Families Program (TANF, formerly Aid to Families with Dependent Children or AFDC) average monthly caseload was 4 million in 2009, down from 14.2 million in 1994. In New York City, the caseload continued to fall after 2005, and was at 350,000 in early 2010.

These dramatic caseload declines inspired a small army of researchers who attempted to explain them. The resulting analyses have not been very satisfying. The declines were far larger than anyone would have predicted from previous history. The econometric studies established the importance of expanding the Earned Income Tax Credit and child support enforcement activities, but they mainly focused on the effects of an extremely good economy and tight labor market. The fact that caseloads have increased very little and in some places continued to fall during the 2007–2009 recession casts some doubt on the power of this latter explanation. Perhaps in desperation, researchers also hypothesized that a change had taken place in the "culture" of the welfare system and in the perceptions of recipients and potential recipients about welfare.

This book is an important contribution to our understanding of what was in fact going on in the welfare system and in related work programs after welfare reform. New York City's welfare system is unusual in many ways. The size, scale, and diversity of the city are huge. Moreover, New York City is governed by New York State's constitutional guarantee of assistance to the needy and by legislation and court decisions that are unusually generous. There is no effective time limit for welfare receipt in New York and only modest financial sanctions for noncompliance with rules. New York guarantees assistance to all, not just to families with children, and the New York caseload is thus unusual in its high proportion of men and of nonparents. But these very differences make New York an interesting place to study what goes on in welfare offices, where the attitudes and behaviors of the workers are almost by definition more important than the federal rules, and where the diverse caseload increases the relevance of the findings to employment programs generally.

New York City refers all employable applicants to work programs and assigns them randomly to sites, which is a boon for researchers. All the programs employ a basic "work-first" strategy, which means that their goal is to place participants in jobs as quickly as possible. This book documents how that strategy is put into practice, how variations on it are developed by individual programs, and how well programs do in achieving their goals. The programs themselves differ in their demographics, size, for-profit or nonprofit status, and structure of performance incentives, as well as in management style and emphasis on different tactics within the basic work-first strategy. Because New York City also has a reasonably good system for tracking participants, it provides an opportunity to study the effects of this variation.

The most sobering finding of this study is undoubtedly the overall placement rate. Of the 20,677 welfare recipients assigned to employment programs, the subjects of this study, only 6 percent were placed in jobs and still employed six months after placement. But of those who showed up and persisted in the program (20 percent of those assigned), almost two-thirds were placed in jobs and of those almost half were employed six months later. This study does not help us understand the 32 percent who never showed up at all or the additional 48 percent who showed up at least once but did not complete the program. Their experiences, like those of the programs' successes, must be part of the explanation for the caseload declines that were continuing during the period of this study—declines that are clearly not explicable by a 6 percent placement rate from employment programs. Perhaps an awareness of the implicit message conveyed by required work-first employment programs had an impact on those who never showed up, contributing either to them succeeding on their own or giving up on the system as a whole. This would be a nice topic for further research on the dramatic change in welfare, the shape and causes of which remain something of a mystery. The detailed descriptions in this book of how programs create a spirit of partnership, get participants job ready, make good placements, and promote employment retention provide hints of how this might work, conveying an expectation about work and a seriousness about pursuing it.

The most important contributions of this book, however, are its insights into what distinguishes the most successful work-first programs from those that have less-good placement and retention rates. Increasing the effectiveness of employment programs is important beyond the narrow confines of the welfare system. Even after the economy recovers from the serious recession it is in as of this writing, many will remain unemployed and out of the labor force, in need of whatever help the employment services system can provide.

The findings of the study are suggestive and relevant beyond both the welfare system and New York City. To some extent they are intuitive and predictable: The most effective programs at placing people quickly into jobs are those that emphasize quick job placement, require immediate job search rather than encouraging job training, focus on job placement rather than case management, and operate under performance incentives that reward quick placement and retention. These results confirm unsurprising findings from the management literature that organizations can indeed get what they measure and that a clear focus on well-defined goals can lead to the achievement of those goals. This appears to be what is going on in these New York City employment programs. The most successful programs are intensely focused on their clients' getting jobs quickly and making sure they stay employed, and they put in place programs and approaches that work toward this goal.

More surprising are the findings about management as distinguished from strategy. Those of us who care about the management of organizations firmly believe that it matters whether organizations are structured and led well. Elements of that would include the right strategy, of course, but they would also include articulating a clear mission, establishing goals consistent with the mission, and monitoring performance. They would also include building a staff team, and motivating and mentoring all staff. We expect that organizations that are managed well along these dimensions will achieve better results. Andy Feldman expected that as well and designed his research to look both at the dimensions of good management and at their relationship to organizational performance.

What he found among the employment programs that he looked at, however, was that the strategic dimensions of organizational leadership were considerably more important than the management dimensions. Programs that had made good strategic decisions about immediate job search and a quick-placement approach were more successful than programs that made other strategic decisions, even if they were not particularly well managed along the standard dimensions. The book provides some evidence that good management can somewhat mitigate the effects of bad strategic decisions. It also offers some insightful diagnoses about why organizations persist in less effective strategies—some because of incomplete information, others because their conceptions of who they are and what they do well are not consistent with quick-placement practices.

The findings and insights in this book should be taken seriously by both designers and managers of employment programs, whether or not they are in New York City or are connected to a welfare system. If nothing else, the sobering overall placement numbers are a reminder of the magnitude of the challenge and the importance of continuous experimentation to try to discover new and better ways of helping people find work. The findings about strategies that do seem to advance quick placements are good reminders that focused strategies aligned with desired measurable outcomes can in fact be effective.

More generally, the book is an important reminder of the power of performance management (you can indeed induce what you measure and pay for) for both potential good and ill. Its reminds us that managers ought to measure and monitor what they care about and provide strategies and incentives that push their organizations toward achieving the results they have decided to focus on and measure. But they also need to think every so often about whether what they are measuring is indeed what they care about and about what they might be missing.

Toward that end, it is worth remembering another aspect of the context of this study. During the 1980s and 1990s, states across the country experimented with a variety of welfare-to-work approaches. A few dozen of these were rigorously evaluated using the methods of random assignment. The nonprofit research firm, MDRC, conducted most of these evaluations, which included cost-benefit analyses. These evaluations found, importantly, that work-first programs, most of which were built around initial mandatory job search, were the most effective in moving people off the welfare rolls—presumably into employment—and saving government money. They tended to be either neutral or only very slightly positive in terms of income gains for the recipients, but their clear effects on the diminution of welfare rolls and government budgets meant that they were widely adopted across the country, including in New York City, and incorporated into the logic behind the welfare reform legislation of 1996. Another important finding of these evaluations was that mandatory education-first approaches had pretty uniformly negative effects both on government budgets and on participants' incomes, at least in the short- to medium-term time frame of the evaluations. This finding seems counterintuitive to many service providers, but it is quite well documented and consistent across studies, and has reinforced what has become the conventional wisdom about the superiority of quick-placement strategies.

Since this first round of welfare-to-work studies, states have experimented with other strategies, with somewhat less clear results. One group of experiments has looked at earnings supplement programs, which have unambiguously positive effects on recipients' incomes and mostly negative effects on government budgets. Other experiments have looked at mixed strategies that try to tailor their interventions to the situations of recipients. Some of these have generated very positive results for both participants and government budgets, and they are clearly worthy of further exploration.

These studies, which are analyzed very well in the 2009 MDRC publication *Welfare-to-Work Program Benefits and Costs*, are important reminders that there is a good deal of high-quality empirical analysis that is relevant to the design of welfare-to-work programs and that some approaches have been clearly demonstrated to dominate others in achieving desired outcomes. Questions of what is right for whom in what circumstances, however, have not been settled. It is crucial that we continue to learn from ongoing comparative evaluations as well as from studies of specific strategies and approaches. This book, I believe, is a fine example of the kind of learning that we need to be engaged in.

Mary Jo Bane
Harvard University

1
Introduction

This book is a case study of how New York City's welfare-to-work programs were managed and implemented in the mid 2000s. New York City's welfare system is unique in many ways, so the results may or may not be generalizable to other cities. Even so, the case study is intended to be a rich source for the generation of hypotheses and a compelling and interesting story in itself.

What makes New York City's welfare system unique? To start, it is the largest urban welfare system in the nation, with about 350,000 individuals receiving cash assistance in early 2010 at a cost of more than $10 million per month.[1] About one in 25 individuals in the national welfare caseload resides in New York City.[2] Another relatively unique feature is the use of private contractors (nonprofit and for-profit organizations) to provide all of the employment services for welfare recipients. A few other cities also use private contractors, including San Diego, Milwaukee, and Houston, but most cities use government agencies to provide welfare-to-work services (Sanger 2003). New York City also stands out because of its use of performance-based contracts, with the providers' compensation tied to job placement and employment retention outcomes of participants, not simply to the number of people served. And finally, the scope of the New York City's welfare benefits is unique. In terms of eligibility, for example, the city (and, in fact, all of New York State) provides benefits to qualifying noncustodial individuals, in addition to qualifying custodial parents and their children. As a result, the city's caseload has a much larger percentage of noncustodial adult men than most other cities. And in terms of time limits, New York City (and State) does not have the typical five-year limit on lifetime benefits. Instead, once custodial recipients exceed five years of cash benefits (or noncustodial individuals exceed two years), they are eligible for a safety-net program without a time limit, paid for with state and local funds.[3]

Two additional unique features of New York City's welfare system are, coincidently, useful from a research perspective. First, 26 welfare-to-work programs operate within the five boroughs in New York City, and the city randomly assigns welfare recipients to different programs within their boroughs.[4] Recipients who live in Brooklyn, for instance, are randomly assigned to one of the eight programs within that borough. The city uses random assignment to be fair to programs, aiming to create an even distribution in terms of participant characteristics. But from a research perspective, this form of assignment creates a natural experiment that reduces selection bias when comparing programs' results. Second, the city gives programs latitude to design their own service strategies, as long as those strategies emphasize a relatively quick entry into jobs. The resulting differences in program practices create useful variation for investigating which practices are more effective than others.

Despite its unique features, New York City's welfare system shares a fundamental similarity—its work-first approach—with almost all other current U.S. welfare systems. Work-first programs use immediate job search, or short-term training followed by job search, rather than longer term education and training. Their goal is to move individuals quickly into unsubsidized employment.

The shift to work first occurred across the nation in the mid 1990s catalyzed by federal welfare reform. In the decade preceding that reform, rigorous evaluations of welfare-to-work programs were interpreted as documenting that work-first (or "labor-force-attachment") programs produced better results than skill-building (or "human-capital-development") programs, including higher employment rates, less welfare usage, and higher incomes (Bloom and Michalopoulos 2001). Influenced by those evaluations and, most importantly, by the new mandates of 1996 Personal Responsibility and Work Opportunity Reconciliation Act (PRWORA), states and localities across the nation adopted a work-first approach.

Today, almost a decade and a half after that sea change in policy and practice, we still know surprisingly little about which frontline practices are most effective within the work-first framework. In other words, why are some work-first programs better able to help welfare recipients become and stay employed? This book aims to provide new insights into that question.

TANF AND OTHER U.S. EMPLOYMENT AND TRAINING PROGRAMS

PRWORA created the Temporary Assistance for Needy Families (TANF) program, established a five-year lifetime time limit on receiving welfare using federal funds, and gave states broad flexibility to design their own TANF programs. It also imposed new requirements on states to connect welfare recipients with work. In particular, states were required to have 50 percent of all families on cash assistance participate in a work activity by 2002 or face financial penalties. In accordance with TANF's work-first emphasis, vocational educational training can count toward work requirements for no more than 12 months and for no more than 30 percent of the caseload. Moreover, all recipients are also required to engage in work within 24 months of receiving cash assistance. In terms of funding, the federal government provides about 65 percent ($16.5 billion in 2009) of TANF funds, while states provide the remainder.[5]

Since the mid 1990s and the passage of PRWORA, the number of welfare recipients in the United States has declined dramatically. After peaking at more than 5 million families in the mid 1990s, the national welfare caseload dropped by more than half, to fewer than 2 million families by 2000.[6] By 2009 there were about 1.7 million families on TANF, but it appeared that the decline had stopped as a result of the recession that began in December 2007. Some states, in fact, saw double-digit percentage increases in 2009.

To situate TANF in a broader context, consider the other main federal employment and job-training policies for adults. They include the Workforce Investment Act (WIA), Trade Adjustment Assistance (TAA), services to veterans, vocational rehabilitation, and adult apprenticeship. Unlike TANF, these policies are not specifically targeted to low-income individuals, but like TANF, they are implemented by states and localities using federal funds.

WIA, which was passed by Congress in 1998, provided $1.3 billion in 2009 to serve more than 300,000 dislocated workers who lost their jobs because of plant closings or mass layoffs. It also provided $900 million to deliver services for 2.7 million adults through One-Stop Career Centers, which are administered by local workforce investment boards. Like TANF, WIA has a work-first emphasis—initial services under WIA focus on job search and career counseling, with education and training only available after efforts to place an individual into a job have failed.

Next, TAA targets workers who lose their jobs because of foreign competition. Established in 1974, it provided almost $1 billion in 2009 for classroom or on-the-job training, job-search assistance, and relocation allowances for trade-dislocated workers. Services to veterans are another element in the federal policy, and they include employment and training assistance for those who are disabled and unemployed, as well as employment workshops for those transitioning back to civilian life. In 2009, the federal government allocated $200 million for employment and training services for veterans. Those services reached more than 850,000 veterans in 2008.

Grants to states for vocational rehabilitation are provided under the Rehabilitation Act of 1973, which provided $2.9 billion in 2009. Services are designed to help individuals with physical or mental disabilities obtain employment and live more independently. They include counseling, medical, and psychological services, job training, and other forms of individualized assistance. Finally, adult apprenticeship offers a combination of on-the-job learning and related instruction in a skilled occupation. Apprenticeship programs are sponsored and operated on a voluntary basis by employers, employer associations, or partnerships between employers and labor unions. Federal funds ($21 million in 2009) are given to states to oversee and enforce federal and state standards for registered apprenticeships. Annually, almost 30,000 apprenticeship program sponsors representing about 225,000 employers offer registered apprenticeship training to more than 300,000 apprentices.

THE NEED FOR BETTER WELFARE-TO-WORK PRACTICES

PRWORA clearly did end welfare as we knew it, but it did not end the need to help low-income Americans gain self-sufficiency and a foothold on the American Dream. The increased unemployment and poverty caused by the deep recession in the late 2000s make that clear, but there are at least two other reasons why improved practices in welfare-to-work services are needed today. One is that many of those who have left the welfare rolls are still poor. High poverty rates among welfare leavers demonstrate the need for more effective policies (for all low-income individuals) to help people move up the economic ladder and to achieve sustained employment. The other reason is that states will soon face new mandates under TANF to place a larger percentage of their welfare recipients in work or job-preparation activities. More effective ways of helping individuals become and stay employed can assist states in meeting that challenge.

Addressing High Poverty Rates among Leavers

Welfare reform, increased financial supports for work through the Earned Income Tax Credit and minimum wage, and the strong economy in the mid to late 1990s combined to produce remarkable success in boosting employment rates among welfare recipients and reducing dependence. For example, the employment rate of never-married mothers over the age of 16 who lived with their own children (those under age 18)—the group most likely to receive public assistance—rose from just under 45 percent in 1993 to over 65 percent by 2000 (Burtless 2004). During the same period, almost three million families moved off the welfare rolls, and poverty rates dropped sharply. The share of single mothers below the poverty line fell by about a fifth between 1995 and 2000, from 36.5 to 28.5 percent, according to the Census Bureau. The poverty rate for this group has since increased to 32.5 percent in 2009, a figure that may continue to increase as a result of the effects of the economic recession from late 2007 to mid-2009.

In short, despite the notable successes of welfare reform, almost a third of single mothers remain poor. Looking specifically at welfare leavers, in fact, poverty rates are even higher. About 40 to 50 percent of leavers are poor (Acs and Loprest 2004). Why are so many leavers poor? One obvious reason is low skills that lead to low wages. A related factor is tension between motherhood and career advancement opportunities, such as returning to school or moving up the job ladder. When faced with a choice between higher wages or control over their schedules, for example, many leavers choose the latter (Seefeldt 2008). A third often-overlooked factor behind leavers' high poverty rates is inconsistent work patterns. The majority of leavers (about three in five) work upon exit from welfare, and four out of five work at some point during the year after exit. Moreover, when leavers are employed, they usually work full time and earn wages several dollars above the federal minimum wage. But many individuals lose their jobs within a few weeks or months of starting, often leading to significant periods of joblessness before they become employed again. In fact, only about 4 in 10 leavers work consistently during the year (Acs and Loprest 2004). Nonwork, in other words, remains an important cause of poverty in the United States, despite the shift to work-oriented welfare policies. Only 11 percent of the working-age poor held full-time, year-round jobs, according to one study (Schwartz 2004). In contrast, only 2.6 percent of all full-time, year-round workers were poor. Fighting poverty among leavers today, therefore, will require finding better ways to help people boost their earnings potential, balance work and family, and achieve greater sustained employment.[7]

Meeting the Challenge of New TANF Rules

Congress reauthorized TANF in 2006, a decade after it became law. In doing so, it significantly toughened TANF's work requirements. Prior to reauthorization, states were required to place half of all single-parent welfare recipients in jobs, or work-readiness activities such as job search, or face financial penalties. There was a loophole, however. States could reduce their work requirements by the percentage by which their welfare caseloads fell after 1995. Because most states experienced large caseload declines in the mid to late 1990s, the majority of states ended up facing no effective work requirement. That changed with reauthorization, which essentially eliminated the caseload reduction credits.[8] This means that states must place a much higher share of their caseloads in work or work-related activities, or else face financial penalties.

Those tougher work requirements are temporarily on hold because of economic weakness. In particular, one provision of the American Recovery and Reinvestment Act of 2009—the federal stimulus bill—is to hold states harmless in terms of work requirements for TANF caseload increases that occur in 2009 through 2011. When that provision expires, states will likely need to boost their work participation rates by between a third and a half. More effective welfare-to-work policies can help states meet those requirements by assisting more people to become and stay employed.

Summary of Findings

To investigate what works within work first, this study focuses on New York City's welfare system, with 16 nonprofit and 3 for-profit organizations operating 26 welfare-to-work programs (or "sites") at the time of this study. These Employment Service and Placement (ESP) programs, as they are called, are paid solely based on performance.[9] Moreover, as noted earlier, they are given broad discretion by the city's welfare department to design and operate their own programs. As a result, although all the programs are work first—all are focused on getting individuals into jobs relatively quickly and none offers longer term education and training—their strategies and practices differ. Readers should be aware, however, that the training-related findings of this study apply only to the type of short-term, classroom-based training used within the city's welfare system, not to longer term education and training or on-the-job training.

Both qualitative and quantitative methods are used in this volume to examine program operations and performance, as described in greater detail in Appendix A. First, field research was conducted from October 2004 to March 2005, including program observations and interviews with 86 staff members. Next, individual-level data were analyzed for the more than 14,000 individuals who participated in one of the 26 programs during the study period, with follow-up data through March 2006. Performance is measured based on programs' abilities to place people into jobs and to have them be still working (at any job, not necessarily the original one) six months later.

Common aspects of work-first programs

Judging from the range of nonprofit and for-profit providers in New York City, today's work-first programs have several aspects in common, beyond the obvious commonality of being work first. Specifically, the programs have four similar components to their service strategies (Figure 1.1). First, all of the programs aim to create a "spirit of partnership" with participants—the staff works to gain participants' trust to facilitate productive working relationships. At the same time, it also

Figure 1.1 Common Elements of Work-First Programs' Service Strategies

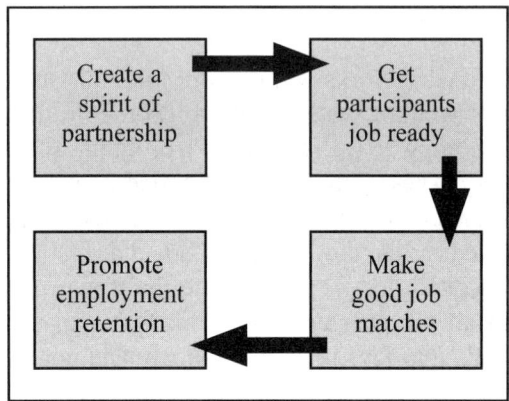

means setting expectations about participants' professionalism while in the program, such as showing up on time and following directions and other rules to help people prepare for the workplace. Creating a spirit of partnership requires a careful balance of trust-building and setting expectations for behavior.

Second, programs help participants become job ready. This often includes preparing people for job interviews through employment-readiness workshops and through case management to help people deal with issues that are preventing them from becoming or staying employed. At some programs, it also includes encouraging and assisting participants to enroll in short-term job training. Training programs typically last a few weeks to three months and are run by private training providers, community colleges, or associations of employers. They include training to be a food service worker, certified nurse's assistant, medical assistant, customer service worker, commercial driver, building maintenance staff, security guard, administrative assistant, and more.

A third commonality is that programs aim to make good job matches by connecting participants with job leads that fit with their skills and interests. This process is usually led by "job developers" who act as intermediaries between participants and employers. Job developers use their existing employer contacts, or hunt for new leads, to maintain an ongoing list of open positions. They then refer participants to job interviews when peoples' abilities and interests match the existing job openings. Although job developers have been part of past welfare-to-work efforts in the United States, the developers in New York City play a somewhat broader role, including screening participants to determine if they are qualified for particular job openings and coaching them before interviews.

Finally, all of the programs provide assistance to those who have gotten jobs to help them stay employed over time. Most commonly, this is done by "retention specialists" who keep in touch with participants after placement, giving them encouragement and advice about workplace or personal issues. They also encourage participants who lose their jobs to return to the programs to be placed in new jobs.

Given these four commonalities, some programs emphasize certain aspects more than others. For example, some providers have more urgency about getting people into jobs quickly and offer only a few days of job-readiness counseling. Others make job readiness a central part of their programs, including encouraging short-term training opportunities and providing substantial case management and multiweek workshops about thriving in the workplace. Different approaches reflect, in part, different views among program leaders about effective practices for facilitating employment. They also reflect different organizational missions among the programs, as well as different staff capacities and skills. For example, some programs have orientation staffs with especially engaging personalities that enable them to create a strong spirit of partnership within the first few days, whereas others do not.

For-profit providers have better overall results

Six of the 26 program sites are run by for-profit organizations, with the remainder being nonprofit, which provides a window into performance by profit status but certainly not a definitive one given the sample size. The results from New York City show that for-profit employment programs achieve higher placement rates than nonprofit ones, although their employment retention rates are lower. In other words, you are more likely to get a job when served by a for-profit program, but once employed you are less likely to keep it. Even so, for-profit programs have better overall results. The total share of participants that becomes employed and is still working (at any job) six months later is higher at for-profits by 25 percent, or two percentage points.

These findings suggest, maybe not surprisingly, that for-profits are more responsive to contractual incentives than nonprofits. This means that, when governments design service contracts with for-profits, they need to be especially careful that financial incentives are aligned with the results they wish to achieve. If agencies are able to specify particular outcomes they wish to maximize, and if they target financial rewards to those outcomes, for-profits will likely be more responsive than nonprofits to those rewards.

Although for-profits perform better, on average, it is worth noting that among the 26 programs in New York City, the top two in terms of overall results are nonprofits. There is no doubt, in other words, that nonprofits can be high-performing organizations. But at least in this sample, the range of performance among nonprofits is wider. In fact, while the top two programs are nonprofits, so are the bottom 12. For-profits, on the other hand, have a narrower range of performance that is centered within the top half of performers.

Programs that are paid fully based on performance do better than those with only partial performance-based pay

New York City uses fully performance-based contracts for all its welfare-to-work programs. The contracts specify that, for every welfare recipient assigned to a program, the program receives one payment if it places the person in a job, a second payment if the person is still working (at any job, not necessarily the original one) three months later, and a third payment if the person is still working (again, at any job) six months later. But a coalition of nine programs pools the revenues from their contracts and operates under a compensation scheme that is only partly performance based. Under their agreement, half of each program's revenue is based on its performance, while the other half is based on cost reimbursement.

The results suggest that stronger financial incentives for performance lead to better outcomes. Programs in the coalition, which receive only partial performance-based pay, have lower job placement rates. Their employment retention rates are also lower, at least for noncustodial individuals, more than half of whom are men in New York City's programs. For custodial individuals, who are mostly women, the effect on employment retention is uncertain. The positive effects of performance incentives are noteworthy given the rarity of performance-based contracting within the social services field in the United States.

Programs that encourage immediate job search are more effective than those that encourage short-term job training prior to job search

Within the context of helping participants become job ready, an important difference among programs relates to job training. At some programs, staff members assess participants' needs and interests and then refer some individuals to short-term training prior to job search, while referring others to immediate job search. This practice has been referred to as a "mixed initial activities approach." At other programs, the staff emphasizes immediate job search for all participants. These two different approaches echo an older debate, prior to the 1996 welfare bill, between advocates of longer term education and training versus advocates of immediate job search. Today, within the context of work first, the range of strategies has narrowed toward the quick-placement end of the spectrum.

The results imply that the more effective approach is immediate job search for all. Programs that send fewer participants to training have higher job-placement rates. Noncustodial individuals who are placed into jobs also have higher employment-retention rates at these quick-placement providers. For custodial individuals, the effect on retention appears to be positive as well, but it cannot be measured precisely.

In one sense, these results are not surprising because past evaluations of welfare-to-work programs have demonstrated the advantage of immediate job search over intensive training or education for welfare recipients (Hamilton 2002). Yet the type of training used in New York City differs from the typical training of the past. It is shorter term, focused on specific job skills, and targeted to those with strong basic skills.[10] This more customized approach to training, however, did not produce more positive outcomes. The use of random assignment and the inclusion of individual-level controls in the analysis make it unlikely that this result stems from selection bias.

These findings are also noteworthy because a mixed initial activities approach was used by two high-profile, successful welfare-to-work programs in the 1990s: Greater Avenues for Independence (GAIN) in

Riverside, California, and Job Opportunities and Basic Skills (JOBS) in Portland, Oregon (Greenberg et al. 2009). The negative results for training in New York City provide evidence, albeit indirectly, that the success of Riverside GAIN and Portland JOBS may not have stemmed from their use of training. This is consistent with analysis by Walker et al. (2003), who attribute these two programs' success to other factors, including caseload demographics. The hope that a mixed initial activities approach would enable training to be a productive service strategy is not supported by the outcomes in New York City.[11]

Why would this type of targeted, short-term training produce worse employment outcomes for welfare recipients? Program leaders and staff in New York City suggested several possible answers. One is that training is often used as a way for participants to avoid work requirements or to continue working off the books, weakening the connection between training and results. Another is that many individuals on welfare may not be well suited to thrive in classroom-based settings, making on-the-job training through employment a more productive option. To paraphrase one program executive, most participants didn't do well in school in the first place, so why put them back in a classroom? Others suggested that the quality of training programs for welfare recipients is often low or "poor education for poor people," as one person put it. Other possible answers exist as well.[12] Determining the actual causal links between training and program results is a worthy area for future research.

The results from New York City highlight the continuing challenge in American poverty policy of designing training options within welfare-to-work services that demonstrably improve program outcomes. Meeting that challenge will require innovation, whether it is redesigning when and how training is delivered or better aligning the content of training with employer demand. The need to help welfare recipients and other low-income individuals increase their job skills—and therefore their wages—is obvious. Finding productive ways to provide that help is the task before us.

Programs that use a quick-placement approach are more effective than those that use a case-management approach, at least for noncustodial individuals

Another difference within the framework of helping participants become job ready relates to case management, meaning helping participants address any barriers to work that are preventing them from becoming or staying employed.[13] Those barriers can include unstable child care, transportation issues, family problems, or apprehension about entering the work world. (Individuals needing more specialized services are referred to other programs, as discussed below.) The effect of case management on welfare recipients' outcomes has not been well studied, especially in the context of work first.

The results from New York City show that programs with more urgency about getting people employed—that is, those that do less case management—are more successful at placing noncustodial individuals in jobs. For custodial individuals, modest amounts of case management can facilitate placements, but more intensive assistance reduces employment outcomes. Longer term results show that fewer noncustodial individuals become employed for at least six months when served by programs with a stronger case-management focus. The effect on custodial individuals is uncertain, but the data suggest, at best, only a small gain in sustained employment from a case-management approach.

Past research has shown mixed evidence about the benefits of personalized attention (Bloom, Hill, and Riccio 2003; Peck and Scott 2005; Riccio and Orenstein 1996). But because welfare caseloads have fallen dramatically in New York City, as elsewhere in the nation, it would be plausible to predict that those still on the rolls would benefit from more individualized help. The evidence does not support that conjecture.

Why might an emphasis on case management be an ineffective strategy for helping welfare recipients connect with work? Past research has not investigated this question, nor did fieldwork within New York City's programs highlight any particular answer. However, program leaders who are proponents of a quick-placement approach argue that discussing people's problems focuses them of their own limitations. Doing that, they said, lowers people's confidence and undermines programs' sense of momentum towards employment. They also noted that knowing which potential barriers to work will actually prevent particular individuals from getting or keeping jobs is difficult to determine. This point is underscored in the research as well (Strawn and Martinson 2000).

Another possibility is that many welfare recipients are more resilient than some might expect, enabling them to overcome their own barriers to work or at least to learn to work around them. That might be particularly true for individuals for whom apprehension about starting work (described by staff as a common occurrence) is the main employment barrier. A quick path into employment may be the best way to deal with that fear.

It is important to note, however, that the findings in this volume do not apply to welfare recipients with the most serious life challenges for whom intensive personalized assistance is likely required to become employed. In New York City, individuals must be deemed "employable" by the city's welfare department before they are assigned to one of the ESP programs. To be employable, individuals must not face a significant barrier to work, including substance abuse, homelessness, limited English skills, illiteracy, domestic abuse, or a physical or mental disability. Individuals with those barriers are referred to specialized employment programs and are excluded from this study's sample.[14] Also, custodial individuals must have child care in place before they are deemed employable, and those who lack child care can receive free vouchers from the city. The majority of welfare recipients in New York City are deemed employable, giving broader applicability to the findings in this volume.

Finally, it is also worth noting that work-first programs do not necessarily need to eschew social work to be effective. In fact, a few high-performing programs have robust case-management components. But case managers at these programs are focused mostly on vocational issues, often addressing immediate barriers to employment, such as making sure the participant has appropriate work clothes. Moreover, they see themselves as an important part of their programs' job placement efforts rather than as a separate case-management component of the program. These high-performing programs' placement speeds were not among the fastest—some had only average speeds—but they maintained a palpable sense of urgency about getting people into jobs. For program leaders, therefore, building teamwork and shared incentives between case managers and job developers is a critical task if programs strive to provide robust job-readiness assistance while still achieving strong results.[15]

Frontline management practices affect performance, but broader strategic decisions matter more

What is the effect of management and leadership on the performance of work-first programs? This question is not formally tested in this study, but fieldwork from New York City suggests some preliminary answers. In particular, the results imply that effective frontline management, such as establishing a clear organizational mission and goals, monitoring performance and operations carefully, and developing a motivated and well-trained staff does boost performance. All else equal, in other words, better managed programs produce better employment outcomes for participants. But the stronger, more evident finding is that broader strategic decisions impact performance more significantly than frontline management practices. For work-first providers, those strategic decisions include whether or not to emphasize training and whether to use a quick-placement or case-management approach.

The results suggest, for example, that programs with effective strategies but weak management practices can do quite well, while those with ineffective strategies but strong management practices are limited to only modest performance. Even programs with insightful, dedicated leaders and motivated staffs were constrained from being top performers if they emphasized both case management and training.

These findings underscore the central role of strategy formation for the successful management and leadership of social programs. To a large extent, it appears, strategy is destiny. Program leaders can boost participant outcomes by improving frontline management practices and by improving program strategies, but especially by doing the latter.

Notes

1. This figure was somewhat higher during the research period of this volume. In 2005, for example, the city had about 400,000 welfare recipients (New York City Human Resources Administration 2009a).
2. The average monthly TANF caseload was 1.7 million in the first half of 2009 (U.S. Department of Health and Human Services 2009). The average monthly Family Assistance caseload (the city's TANF cases) was approximately 68,000 during the

same period (New York City Human Resources Administration 2009b).
3. In this program, a portion of the grant is paid directly to recipients' landlords, another portion is paid to the utility company, a small amount of cash is provided ($86 per month), and the rest is put on a debit card that can be used at stores that have the equipment to accept that card. State funds are used because federal regulations prohibit federal funds from being used to pay for benefits after an individual has exceeded five years on welfare.
4. Anecdotally, the city sometimes grants requests by individuals who wish to attend certain programs, but it appears that most assignments are random. See Appendix A for further details.
5. All years in this section refer to fiscal years. Moreover, allocated amounts in this section do not include additional funds provided by the American Recovery and Reinvestment Act of 2009, including $5 billion a year in emergency TANF funds for 2009 and 2010.
6. That decline has been attributed to a combination of factors, including the effect of TANF, a strong economy in the second half of the 1990s, and increases in supports for low-wage workers such as increases in the federal minimum wage and the Earned Income Tax Credit (Council of Economic Advisers 1999).
7. In terms of promoting sustained employment, research to date on employment retention efforts for the poor have shown limited success (Scrivener, Azurdia, and Page 2005; Wavelet and Anderson 2002). The results underscore the need for further policy innovations in this area.
8. The reauthorized legislation changed the base year of the credits from 1995 to 2005. Since significant caseload declines have not occurred since 2005, the caseload reduction credits have been much smaller than they were before reauthorization.
9. Specific contractual pay points and dollar amounts are discussed in Chapter 2.
10. This is because Human Resource Administration rules about training vouchers specify that individuals must have decent scores on their basic skills tests (taken by every participant upon arrival into a program) to qualify for a voucher.
11. To obtain definitive answers about the effectiveness of the mixed initial activities approach, impact evaluations would need to directly test this approach against a quick-placement approach. Evaluations of Portland and Riverside did not conduct head-to-head tests of these programs against a quick-placement approach.
12. Another possibility is that programs that encourage training may be using other practices that are the actual source of the performance shortfall. For example, emphasizing training as an option for participants might weaken a program's sense of urgency about becoming employed for its whole caseload, even if only a small fraction of participants actually enters training.
13. The term "case management" is used rather than "social work" because most case managers are not licensed social workers.
14. Individuals needing specialized services are typically identified when they apply for welfare at their Job Centers. The extent of these targeted services in New York City is relatively unique in the United States. For more information on the city's specialized employment programs, see Nightingale (2005).

15. The challenge of creating teamwork is analogous to an older challenge within welfare systems of integrating eligibility staff with employment staff. In New York City, Job Centers do all the eligibility determination, while the for-profit and nonprofit employment programs provide all the employment services. But this study shows that within employment programs, staff can still become bifurcated. In this case, the bifurcation is between case managers and job developers. Tension between these roles was apparent at several programs. One site had even recently hired a consultant to get both groups of employees working more productively together.

2
Welfare to Work in New York City

New York City's welfare system is one of the most interesting and important welfare systems in the nation. Although it shares a work-first emphasis with practically every other state and local welfare system today, it also has several unique features, as described in the previous chapter. These include its size, partial privatization, and pay-for-performance contracts with employment programs. We turn next to a more detailed examination of the system's key features, followed by an overview of how welfare-to-work programs within the system operate and a discussion of the programs' results.[1]

KEY FEATURES

Partial Privatization

Nonprofit and for-profit organizations in the city provide all of the employment services for welfare recipients. But unlike some other cities that have used privatization, such as Milwaukee, public-sector employees in New York City maintain a significant role. In particular, the city's Human Resources Administration (HRA) operates welfare offices around the city, called Job Centers, where individuals apply for benefits and have their eligibility verified. Job Center staff members also help individuals secure (and pay for, if needed) child care so that they can begin the employment process.

During the period of this study, from 2004 to 2006, individuals with pending applications for assistance were assigned to one of six Skills Assessment and Job Placement providers (SAPs). These employment programs, run by private contractors, taught job-readiness skills and provided job-search assistance to first-time applicants for welfare.[2] Individuals who did not become employed after two months were assigned to an ESP program, which was also run by private contractors. Nineteen organizations ran 26 ESP sites in the city during this period (Table 2.1). They included for-profit corporations such as America Works and Affiliated Computer Services (ACS), large nonprofit organizations such as Goodwill Industries and Wildcat Service Corporation, and several smaller community-based nonprofits.[3] Compared to SAPs, ESPs had caseloads that were more representative of the national welfare caseload because they serve ongoing welfare cases rather than just new applicants. They are the focus of this volume, and references hereafter to programs, contractors, providers, and sites all refer to ESPs.

Pay-for-Performance Contracts

As noted earlier, the city compensates employment programs on a pay-for-performance basis. The three main pay points, or milestones, that were used are shown in Figure 2.1, along with bonuses that are available if participants achieve certain wage levels and if their welfare cases are closed. As the dollar amounts imply, two-thirds to three-fourths of the potential compensation per participant is tied to employment retention, as opposed to simply job placement. Both the use of pay-for-performance contacts and their focus on retention are relatively unique among welfare systems.

Figure 2.1 Performance Payments for Employment Programs (per participant)

> **Initial job placement:** $1,227 (job must be at least 20 hours per week)
>
> **Employed at the 3-month mark after initial placement:** $2,209 ($2,700 if job is "high wage," defined as $344 per week or more)
>
> **Employed at the 6-month mark after initial placement:** $491 ($1,473 if welfare case is also closed)

NOTE: Dollar amounts are sample payments for one ESP. Payment amounts vary slightly between programs.

Table 2.1 Employment Services and Placement (ESP) Programs

Contractor	Borough
America Works[a]	Bronx
America Works[a]	Queens
America Works[a]	Manhattan
Borough of Manhattan Community College	Manhattan
Career and Education Consultants[a]	Brooklyn
Career and Education Consultants[a]	Staten Island
Catholic Charities	Bronx
Center for Family Life	Brooklyn
Citizens Action Bureau	Bronx
Cypress Hills Local Development Corp.	Brooklyn
East New York Development Corp.	Brooklyn
FEGS	Bronx
Goodwill Industries	Brooklyn
Goodwill Industries	Bronx
Goodwill Industries	Queens
Harlem Congregations for Community Improvement	Manhattan
Henry Street Settlement	Manhattan
Laguardia Community College	Queens
New York City College of Technology	Brooklyn
New York Job Partners[a]	Brooklyn
Northern Manhattan Improvement Corp.	Manhattan
NYANA	Brooklyn
St. Nicholas Neighborhood Preservation Corp.	Brooklyn
WHEDCo	Bronx
Wildcat Service Corp.	Bronx
Wildcat Service Corp.	Manhattan

[a] For-profit.

Accountability Tools: JobStat and VendorStat

To oversee the performance of contractors, HRA took the accountability tool used by New York City's police department, known as CompStat, and adapted it to the welfare-to-work field. In doing so, HRA created "JobStat" and "VendorStat." In JobStat, directors of the Job Centers (the city-run welfare offices) periodically come before HRA leaders to review performance measures and discuss ways of improving results (Sherwood 2005). VendorStat, on the other hand, focuses on the 26 employment programs. Twenty different performance measures are reviewed for each program during VendorStat meetings, including comparisons between a program's performance and the average for all the programs.[4] These two "stat" systems ensure that performance is reviewed on a regular basis for both welfare offices and employment programs.[5]

Public Service Jobs ("Workfare")

New York City is among a handful of cities with workfare programs, meaning that welfare recipients are required to work in public service jobs in return for their welfare grants (Besharov and Germanis 2004; Clark 2005). New York's version is called the Work Experience Program (WEP), and it involves about 15,000 welfare recipients who work in WEP jobs at city agencies or nonprofits three days a week. The other two days are spent at their employment programs.

The WEP program has been a controversial aspect of the city's welfare system, particularly in the mid 1990s when the mayor at the time, Rudolph Giuliani, began requiring all able-bodied, unemployed welfare recipients to participate in workfare jobs. To critics, the WEP program forces welfare recipients to work at often menial, low-skill tasks such as cleaning parks without being paid a regular wage, although participants do receive their welfare benefits. Proponents, on the other hand, argue that workfare jobs help people prepare for a regular work schedule and that doing these jobs encourages people to move into regular wage-paying jobs given that the alternative is unpaid work.

Relatively Lenient Sanctions and Time Limits

New York State's constitutional guarantee of aid to the poor restricts the city from imposing strong sanctions for noncompliance and from establishing a time limit on assistance for families with children. Most states use full-family sanctions, meaning that noncompliance can lead to a termination of all welfare benefits (Bloom and Winstead 2002). New York, on the other hand, imposes partial-family sanctions that lead to benefit reductions but not terminations of aid. As noted earlier, it also does not have a time limit on welfare benefits—a policy shared by only a few states, including California. Families in New York who reach the five-year federal time limit can enter a state- and locally-funded safety-net program.

Those at the frontlines—the staff and leaders of the employment programs—have differing views of these relatively lenient policies. Some see them as an important safety net for the most vulnerable in society, preventing women and children from becoming homeless and destitute. Others see the policies are overly permissive, facilitating joblessness and dependency. In particular, some criticize the fact that individuals who drop out of their programs are, in many cases, reassigned to new programs (or sometimes the same ones) without incurring any penalties. Regardless of one's view, limited administrative authority makes the city especially challenging for employment programs. Weak sanction policies make it more difficult for staff to discourage people from dropping out of their programs, and the lack of a time limit on welfare benefits reduces participants' sense of urgency about becoming employed.

Eligibility for Custodial and Noncustodial Individuals

Welfare recipients in the United States are mostly custodial single mothers because most welfare systems limit eligibility for benefits to low-income individuals with custodial children. In New York City, however, noncustodial poor individuals can also qualify for benefits. If they do, they are required to participate in employment programs just as custodial individuals are. As a result, about 40 percent of employment programs' participants are noncustodial individuals and about 30 percent of the recipients are male. Nationally, less than 10 percent of welfare recipients are male.[6]

WHAT EMPLOYMENT PROGRAMS DO: AN OVERVIEW

The 26 employment programs range in size considerably, with the smallest receiving about 15 new participants every two weeks and the largest receiving 175 every two weeks.[7] Some participants stay for only a few days, either because they get placed in jobs or because they drop out of their programs. Others stay for several weeks or months. Programs can work with participants for up to six months before they are randomly reassigned to another program.

All of the programs have an orientation period that lasts for a day or two. During orientation, participants learn about the program, meet with case managers to create an employment plan, and take a skills test. (The employment plan and skills test are required by the city.) Individuals who are deemed immediately job ready are usually fast-tracked and sent on job interviews within a few days. Staff estimated that about 10 percent of participants are job ready at program entry.

Following orientation, participants attend job-readiness workshops that last from a few days to about two weeks. Workshop topics typically include how to apply and interview for jobs, what to expect in terms of workplace norms of behavior, and transitional benefits and work supports that are available such as the Earned Income Tax Credit. When not in workshops, individuals meet with case managers to address any barriers to work that may be preventing them from getting or keeping jobs. Individuals with significant barriers are usually screened out prior to arriving at the programs, but in cases where staff members become aware of significant barriers, programs can deassign individuals by referring them back to their Job Centers for further evaluation.

Participants also meet with job developers either at the start of the program or, at some programs, after case managers have deemed participants "job ready," a process that can take anywhere from a day to a few weeks or longer. Job developers are in charge of building and maintaining employer contacts to provide job leads to participants. They also assess participants' fit with particular job openings and refer them to job interviews.

Some participants are referred to short-term training before they are sent on job interviews. Programs can request HRA training vouchers for some participants.[8] If a request is approved, the participant is given a $1,500 voucher that can be used at any of the dozens of private training providers in the city. Voucher-eligible training usually lasts from a few weeks to three months. About 5 percent of all participants receive these vouchers. Some participants also receive free training from employer-sponsored programs. This type of training is sometimes called "certificate training," since graduates receive a certificate showing that they are qualified to be, for example, a security guard or home-health aid.

System-wide data on the use of employer-sponsored training are not available, but anecdotal evidence indicates that employment programs that use more voucher training also tend to use more free employer-sponsored training.

After spending two weeks, full time, at their employment programs, individuals who have not yet become employed start a new schedule, spending two days a week at their employment programs and three days a week at WEP (workfare) jobs.

Participants who become employed are eligible for two-week subway passes, paid for by HRA, for up to six months. They are required to pick up those passes at their employment programs every two weeks.[9] This provides an incentive for participants to return to their programs on a regular basis so that staff can interact with them—asking them how their jobs are going, providing encouragement, and determining if they need any help to stay employed.

People who are placed in jobs and then lose those jobs have two options. Some choose to go back to their Job Centers and request that their full welfare benefits be reinstated. In that case, they are randomly assigned again to an employment program. Others return to their previous employment programs for help in getting another job. Programs encourage individuals to choose the latter option because it gives the programs the opportunity to find participants new jobs prior to their three- or six-month retention milestone dates. Recall that programs get paid for retention as long as people are working at any job on those milestone dates.

Program Performance

The outcomes for welfare recipients served by the 26 employment programs are summarized in Figure 2.2. About 68 percent (14,000) of the 20,677 people assigned to the programs during the study period showed up for at least a day.[10] The roughly one-third that fails to show up may face benefit cuts unless they request a new start date and begin to attend a program.

Among those who begin attending their employment programs, some are deassigned by the staff because of significant barriers to work. After deassignments, about 60 percent of those initially assigned are still participating. Many of these individuals either drop out or, less

Figure 2.2 Outcomes for Individuals Assigned to Employment Programs

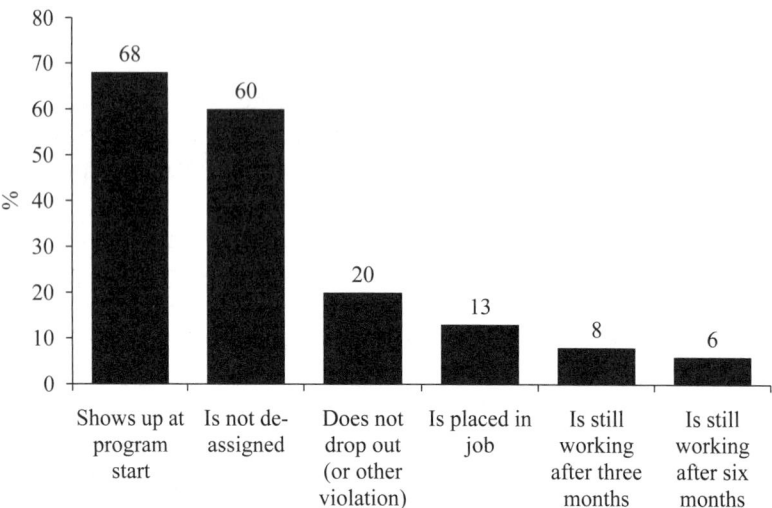

commonly, violate other program rules, resulting in termination from their employment programs and possible HRA sanctions.[11] In fact, about half of all participants drop out during the first week, and only 20 percent of those assigned to programs show up, are not deassigned, and are not terminated.

Among the latter group of "active participants" (meaning people who go through the programs), almost half became employed. But, as the figure shows, this group of placed participants represents only 13 percent of the total number initially assigned. In fact, only 8 percent of assigned individuals become employed and are still working (at any job) three months after placement—a figure that drops to 6 percent at the six-month mark.

To some observers and community advocates, these outcomes represent "a failure of this work-first model in achieving its main goal—moving people from welfare to work, into jobs and towards economic independence" (Youdelman 2005). According to this view, the fact that only 13 percent of assigned individuals become employed, and even fewer keep those or other jobs, is a sign that people need more intensive help, including more opportunities for education and training.[12]

From a different perspective, though, one could see these results as quite strong, given the policy context. New York State's mild sanction policy and its lack of a time limit on aid likely contribute to widespread noncompliance. Two-thirds of those assigned to employment programs never show up, drop out, or violate program rules. The job placement and retention rates of those who do actively participate are much higher. Figure 2.3 shows that among those who show up, are not deassigned, and are not terminated, 62 percent become employed. Moreover, the six-month retention rate among placed participants (47 percent, not shown in the figure) is higher than that of a well-known employment program in Chicago, Project Match. At that program, which provides long-term, individualized employment services to welfare recipients, 40 percent of placed participants are still working after six months (Olson, Berg, and Conrad 1990).

How do the employment outcomes from New York City compare to other cities? Data are limited on this question, but one piece of evidence comes from a comparison of outcomes of single mothers (not necessarily those on welfare) in New York City with the average for other U.S. central cities from the mid 1980s to early 2000s (O'Neill and Korenman 2005). Throughout the period, the share of single mothers on welfare was higher in New York City than the national average, while the share that was employed was lower. It appears, though, that the employment

Figure 2.3 Outcomes for Active Program Participants

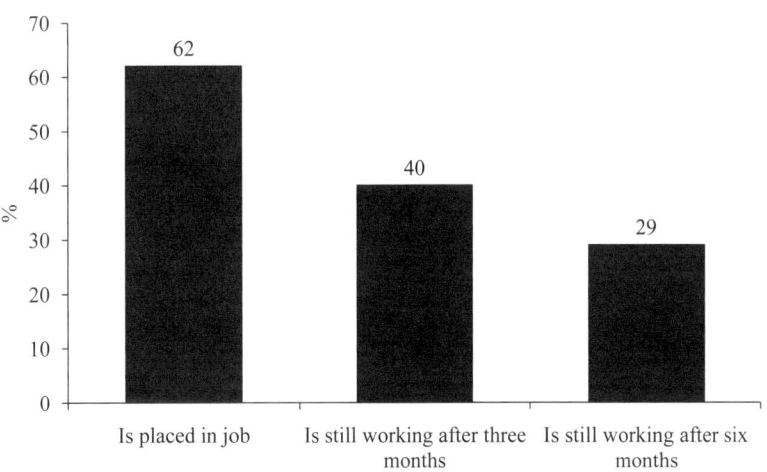

NOTE: "Active" is defined as participants who show up for at least a day, are not deassigned, and are not sanctioned.

rate of single mothers in the city grew closer to the national average in the late 1990s (O'Neill and Korenman 2005).

Recall that program performance in this book was measured in the mid 2000s, when the economy was growing modestly and labor markets were relatively tight. Another question is whether program performance would be lower today, given the continued effects of the national economic recession from 2007 to 2009. Theoretically, the effect of economic weakness on program performance could be either positive or negative, on balance. For example, in a weak economy there are obviously fewer job openings, making job placement more difficult, all else equal. But economic weakness also tends to bring more advantaged individuals into the welfare caseload, including those with more skills, education, and recent work experience. The data from New York City suggest, in fact, that these two factors may have largely balanced each other out. Job placement rates among welfare recipients remained fairly constant from 2006 through 2009, with a slight increase during the period.[13]

Notes

1. A key feature of New York City's welfare system, its specialized employment services for hard-to-serve participants, was discussed in Chapter 1 and is not discussed further in this chapter.
2. In 2006, after the period of this study, HRA eliminated the separate programs for new applicants and combined the SAPs and ESPs into what it now calls "Back to Work" providers.
3. In 2003, ACS acquired the welfare-to-work services business of Lockheed Martin, best known as a defense contractor.
4. Performance measures include the percentage of participants who become employed by the end of 4, 13, and 26 weeks of the programs; the average wage of placed participants and recidivism rates back onto welfare; employment retention rates; and process measures such as the share of participants who have worked with a case manager to complete an "employment plan." Also, note that the use of random assignment of participants to programs, within boroughs, helps city administrators (and programs) compare VendorStat performance data across programs. The city's decision to use random assignment was not related to VendorStat, but it had the effect of making VendorStat data much more straightforward to interpret, given that programs have a more even distribution (within boroughs) of participants in terms of measured and unmeasured characteristics.
5. These tools are supplemented by other measures, including periodic random HRA

audits of welfare recipients' case files to ensure that Job Centers and employment programs are adequately serving individuals.
6. The city's inclusion of noncustodial individuals may be ahead of its time given the seemingly growing focus in the United States on efforts to reduce prison recidivism among ex-felons, a population that is mainly low-income, noncustodial men. Since employment programs involving low-income men are relatively rare, New York City provides insights into serving that population. The results presented in Chapter 9 show that men in the city's programs had similar employment outcomes as women. This is contrary to what may be conventional wisdom in the United States that poor males have weaker results than poor females in employment programs.
7. These data pertain to the average number of people that show up for at least one day to their programs.
8. Requests for training vouchers must show that the participant has good attendance at their employment program, that they have the necessary basic skills to receive the training desired, and that there is a cogent rationale for needing training.
9. Some programs shift to a monthly pickup schedule after people have been employed for a few months.
10. The fact that about one-third of assigned individuals do not show up to their programs raises the possibility of selection effects. To investigate this issue, quantitative results were run using alternative sample definitions, including anyone assigned to a program, whether or not they showed up. The results were fairly consistent across sample definitions and none of the main findings of the volume would change using alternative sample definitions. The case for defining the sample as participants (those who show up for at least a day) is also stronger if program characteristics (other than geographic location) are uncorrelated with whether people show up. Only one program characteristic was correlated with show rates, deassignment rate. When two outliers in terms of this characteristic were removed, however, even this variable became uncorrelated.
11. Those who are terminated may face benefit cuts unless they show good cause in conciliation meetings with HRA. If they show good cause (which anecdotally is fairly easy), they are randomly assigned to an employment program again.
12. A lack of jobs might be another factor in these low employment rates, although during the study period in the mid 2000s, that did not appear to be the case. Staff at employment programs typically said that there were enough jobs for participants.
13. The data show that about 1.7 percent of all Family Assistance and Safety Net recipients were placed in jobs per month during early 2006, a figure that rose to about 2 percent by the end of 2009. These data pertain to placements among all welfare recipients in the city, not just those who participated in employment programs, so they are not directly comparable to the placement rates discussed in this chapter. Even so, they show no major shift in placement rates as the economy weakened in the later 2000s (author's calculation based on total placements and caseload size from New York City Human Resource Administration 2009b).

Part 1

Shared Strategic Elements among Work-First Employment Programs

3
Creating a Spirit of Partnership

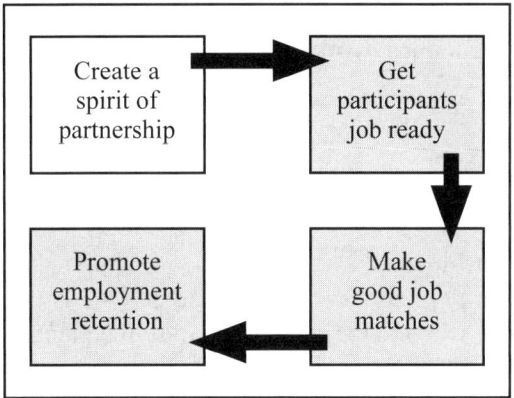

The first common element among today's welfare-to-work programs, judging from the range of programs in New York City, is what I call "creating a spirit of partnership." It involves staff working to develop productive working relationships with new participants. This usually occurs during program orientation, which lasts a day or two. As a result, orientation staff members play a central role in creating a spirit of partnership. The task of maintaining that spirit is then handed off to others, including case managers and job developers, who work with participants after orientation.

Successfully establishing a sense of partnership is not a simple task. It is multifaceted and requires staff with strong interpersonal skills. Participants must see that the organization and its staff are concerned with their well-being, which is important in building trust. Participants need to be convinced that the program will be useful in improving their lives. Doing this engages participants in the program or, at a minimum, reduces the chances that they will drop out. And finally, establishing a sense of partnership includes setting expectations in terms of participants' professional behavior such as showing up on time, dressing professionally, and following directions. Setting these expectations gives people practice with workplace norms, something that is particularly important for those who have been out of work for longer periods of time.

The term "partnership" reflects two emphases—what the staff does for participants and what the staff expects of participants. There is a simultaneous pull and push to the dynamic. The "pull" is about building trust and emphasizing the program's usefulness.[1] The "push" is about requiring people to meet workplace norms.[2]

RATIONALE

Program staff members explained that the pull side of the spirit of partnership is important for several reasons. One is that participants, especially those who are longer term welfare recipients, are aware that they can drop out of their employment programs and usually avoid HRA sanctions by getting reassigned to a new program. People are more likely to drop out if they do not feel a connection with the staff or if they believe the program will be a waste of time. As a site director explained, "Trust is a huge issue because if they don't trust us, they're not going to want to stay."

Another reason for building trust is that participants often enter the programs angry about being required to attend. When asked whether participants knew they could be sanctioned by HRA if they did not attend, a case manager explained: "They know for sure. That's part of the reason why they don't want to come from the beginning or why they may be a bit upset when having to come someplace . . . because it's just a threat that hangs over their heads." Newer welfare recipients are more fearful of being sanctioned than long-term recipients because the latter group knows how to "play the system."

Other participants are angry or distrustful because they feel they have been treated poorly at the Job Centers (the city-run welfare offices), at other employment programs they have attended, or by society in general. As one staff member commented, "They do not come in here wanting to give you even that slightest bit of trust. They come in here with a lot of bad thoughts . . . because they figure 'I'm on welfare. I'm just on the bottom of the pit.' And they feel like they get treated that way wherever they go."

Personal problems can be another source of anger. Some people are frustrated, a job developer explained, "not [being] able to get a job to provide for their family. They have problems with their family. They have problems with their children. It's a lot of things."

By gaining people's trust and emphasizing that the program can help them, staff members try to reduce dropout rates and form productive working relationships with participants. One orientation facilitator noted that she can assess how well she conducts the first day's orientation session by the turnout rate on the second day. Another explained, "Once they come here, I think we have control over whether they come back or not . . . [It's] the way we present ourselves. First impressions are important."

The push aspect of partnership involves setting expectations and rules about workplace norms. One reason programs do this is to prepare people for work by replicating (at least to some extent) a workplace environment. As a case manager explained:

> Our program functions as a mirror of how they will be expected to function in the world of work. The program is nine to five because most jobs are nine to five. You are expected to be here on time. You are expected to come here and manage your time—your transportation and commute here—to follow a schedule. This hopefully will prepare you as a warm up to your job.

Another rationale for professional standards is that it helps staff members determine who is job ready and who needs more coaching. If someone consistently shows up late to a program, for example, they are unlikely to arrive on time to a job. Moreover, if the staff refers participants to jobs and if (assuming they are hired) those individuals do not perform well because of poor behavior, programs can hurt their relationships with those employers.

A third reason to enforce work norms is to help create more order within programs. Without rules about attendance, for example, people would "fall through the cracks," one site director explained. "We run a very tight ship here, and we have to or else you lose control." Finally, programs enforce rules to push people to take greater responsibility for their actions. For example, a director explained why she puts people on probation (meaning at risk of being removed from the program) if they start to miss job-training classes:

> I put them on probation [and say,] "if you want your [training] certificate, it's not going to be handed out to you because you were here four or five days. You have to earn that. So what kept you away?" They'll say "I don't know. I just didn't feel good." [I'll say,] "Well I didn't feel good either but I was here." . . . When you give them those doors [opportunities to improve], they'll come back and say thank you. You see the thank you notes? [She points to her wall] "Thank you. If you had not stayed on my case I would not have finished that. Thank you for really telling me I had to be disciplined with my time and my personal life." They come back and thank me. That's the tough love.

TECHNIQUES

Creating a spirit of partnership involves blending several messages to build trust, demonstrate programs' usefulness, and set expectations about behavior. One orientation facilitator, in fact, used the term "partnership" to describe the process:

> [I tell them:] "I'm not their friend . . . I'm your partner . . . We're going to partner together to try to seek employment . . . That's what the first part of orientation is. What can you expect from your time here and what can I expect from you when it comes to partnership. You can get 100 percent from me, but I want 100 percent from you."

Another program director noted:

> Our famous line is "If you don't quit on us, we won't quit on you." But there are guidelines we need to follow and we give them all of the guidelines . . . Someone described it as tough love. That's what we try to do here. Professional standards—we're strict. If you work with us, we can get you to the next level.

Building Trust

By building trust, staff members hope to gain participants' cooperation and interest in the programs. As a site director explained, "They are not coming in on a voluntary basis . . . What we hope happens is that as they get to know us and trust us and see exactly what it is we do, that then they would want to come in [and] get engaged and be part of the program."

Giving individual attention during orientation

One way to build trust is through individual attention during the first few days of a program. This helps demonstrate the staff's interest in people's well-being. In the words of one staff member, "When you get to a place and you're frustrated, but then you get that individual attention, you're like 'Oh, yes, somebody can relate to me. Somebody really cares.'" Many programs have one-on-one meetings with participants during the first day or two.

Emphasizing empathy and a desire to help

Some individuals arrive with confrontational attitudes, but showing empathy and a willingness to help can ameliorate that negativity and build trust. One way of doing that is by having orientation staff members share their own experiences of financial struggle or of moving from welfare to work. "Some of us have personal stories on public assistance," a job developer explained, "and sometimes it helps the client to know that you do know what they're going through."

Demonstrating Programs' Usefulness

Another set of practices to build partnership is aimed at convincing participants of the program's usefulness, particularly in terms of connecting them with jobs.

Pitching the program on the first day

As with building trust, the first day is critical for demonstrating a program's value and, in doing so, reducing dropout rates. One orientation facilitator explained to new arrivals, "We only get paid once you get a job, so we're really partners in this whole activity." Her goal, she said, was to "let them know that there are real jobs available, real opportunities . . . If, in that first day, the great majority of the group can believe that they can have success here if they do their part, then by the second day they're ready [to engage]."

Conducting useful and engaging workshops

All of the programs conduct job-readiness workshops, sometimes starting on the first or second day and lasting from a few days to about two weeks. Although their primary purpose is to get people job ready, workshops also signal program quality, based on the usefulness of the information presented. A program director explained, "It's important to put the right person in front of that classroom because, if you don't, people aren't going to come back. They feel that they're wasting their time . . . So you have to put someone there that can relate to the clients in the room." A few programs also had former participants who are now employed talk to new groups during orientation and vouch for the value of the program.

Demonstrating employer connections

Another way programs show their usefulness to new participants is by describing current job leads. For example, one director described how, during orientation, her job developers list the types of jobs that people in previous cohorts have gotten in recent weeks. The goal, she said, was to get people thinking, "Wow, if I stay here for two or three days, I'm actually going to get a shot at an interview." Emphasizing job leads also helps reduce the negative expectations that some participants have. Those expectations, in the words of a workshop facilitator, include the belief that, "They're not going to really have any jobs for me and what they do have is going to be at McDonalds."

Enforcing Workplace Norms

The final technique used to build partnership is enforcing workplace norms. All of the programs discuss rules about professional behavior, although the level of emphasis varies. For example, some programs are strict from the start, while others phase in enforcement over time to provide an adjustment period. Either way, enforcing professional norms while simultaneously building trust requires that rules are set and enforced in a way that the participants will accept. One approach is to model respectful behavior. A workshop facilitator explained:

> We believe words are powerful. If you want someone to behave in a certain way, you have to show that behavior. I'll say "thank you

very much," "excuse me." I don't allow outbreaks in the classroom ... There's a whole reconditioning the first couple of days. I hate using that word, but I think that's what that is—reconditioning to be treated a different way.

Another technique is to downplay hierarchy. For example, one director said members of her staff use themselves as examples, emphasizing how they have to show up to work on time everyday. The message, she said, was, "The world is not requiring something different from you than from me." Staff also spoke about showing leniency if people appear to be legitimately trying to meet expectations. "You've got to show the compassionate side," one case manager noted, "so they say, 'They're pushing me for a reason.'"

VARIATION IN APPROACHES

Engagement

Programs differ in their emphases on trust and engagement, as well as in their abilities to achieve them. In fact, a few workshop facilitators appeared to create more frustration for participants than engagement. One program, for instance, was disorganized and kept participants waiting in a classroom for an hour before the workshop facilitator arrived. At a different program, a facilitator ran a session using true/false questions related to basic workplace norms, but the information was confusing and contradictory and ended up visibly frustrating people. At still another program, the facilitator was too meek to control the group during a skills-assessment workshop. Some participants began to ignore the facilitator and, in fact, started sharing job leads with each other.

At the other end of the spectrum, some programs were especially skilled at engagement. One had several job developers discuss their current job leads during orientation, with participants noticeably interested and asking follow-up questions. Others had staff with impressive abilities to connect with people and to convey useful information. One workshop facilitator, for instance, blended humor, encouragement, professionalism, and an extensive list of tips on becoming and staying employed. She urged participants to take available jobs and then move up over time. In doing so, she described how she had moved from a fast-food cashier as a new émigré from Jamaica to (after six different jobs) a professional:

> I remember there were times after hearing so many "no's" and the tears would be coming down my face. And I'm like "God, am I ever going to find a job?" . . . But I had to take baby steps. I started out at Arby's restaurant . . . [Eventually the manager] said to me "Miss [first name], I can't stand my bookkeeper." She said "I'm going to train you to be my bookkeeper" because she liked my *attitude* and she saw that I was a *team player* . . . [You see,] there are certain qualities that God has blessed you with. [Participants acknowledge: "Uh huh."] . . . So what I need you to do is to *take what you have* and let it work for you until the type of position that you're really looking for comes along. [Italics are emphases of the speaker.][3]

Finally, one nonprofit program took a unique approach to participant engagement. According to the director, the program tries not to be too engaging during the first few days of the program. For example, the staff purposely does not meet one-on-one with participants until the third day, nor does the director want staff to encourage unmotivated people to stay:

> In effect it's two days of probation. If they begin violating [rules] the first two days [e.g., not showing up], it's a good sign that they have a poor prognosis . . . From a business point of view, it's good [if they drop out]. They're showing me that this is someone that's going to do it [drop out] anyway and I'm saving staff labor if they do it on the first week. I'm not going to make it easy on them or try to sell them on being here . . . Part of being job ready is the desire to work.

Fieldwork showed that the program's orientation is average (not low) in terms of engagement. Even so, this program's approach could be considered "creaming," meaning focusing on the most job-ready individuals. The director noted, in fact, "There's a tremendous pressure to cream." But looking at the program's performance, its placement rates (among all participants, not just those who remained after the unofficial probation period) are in the top third of the 26 programs. And its placement rate for long-term welfare recipients is sixth highest.[4] These results suggest that creating strong engagement at the start of a program is not essential—even if it is still helpful—to achieving relatively strong employment outcomes.

Setting Expectations about Work Norms

All programs set expectations about behavior, but some are stricter about enforcing rules than others. According to staff at more lenient programs, leniency gives people time to adjust to new expectations, and flexibility about attendance allows people to take care of personal matters before they begin employment. "We're starting to get harder on the rules," a case manager explained. "But that's not our focus . . . I feel like people know this is not a job . . . If they need to go to doctors' appointments, they bring us the documentation, but that wouldn't work on the job necessarily. But if you can get those appointments out of the way while you're with us before you start working, maybe that's [helpful]." At a few programs, in fact, there was noticeable disagreement among the staff about how strictly to enforce workplace norms. The result was a confusing message for participants and conflict among staff.

Notes

1. In the welfare-to-work field, the concept of engagement has not been closely examined. One reason may be that, until the 1990s, many welfare-to-work programs in the United States served mostly voluntary populations for whom engagement was less of a concern. With participation mandates increasing, especially since the 1996 welfare reform bill, engagement is a more salient issue. One area where engagement has been examined more thoroughly is in child welfare services, where participation is mostly mandatory. Based on a survey of the literature, Dawson and Berry (2002) find that program success in family preservation and other outcomes is linked to families' early cooperation and engagement in services, as well as to caseworkers' ability to develop empathy, trust, and respect with participants. A way to promote engagement, according to another study, is to provide simple and effective services at the beginning of the treatment relationship so that some progress is made quickly (Lewis 1991).
2. In terms of research on enforcing workplace norms of behavior, studies have not examined the link between that emphasis and performance. But Strawn and Martinson (2000) note, "Several successful programs, such as the Center for Employment Training in San Jose, believe strongly in the importance of having a work-like environment, with participants punching time clocks, having a dress code, treating their instructors and peers with respect, and adhering to other standards

of the workplace. Participation in pre-employment services then becomes a 'dress rehearsal' for work." Research also demonstrates that a failure to meet workplace norms on the job is a prime cause of job loss among low-income workers (Berg, Olson, and Conrad 1991; Hershey and Pavetti 1997; Holzer and Wissoker 2001).
3. Interestingly, organizations that run multiple sites did not always show consistency in terms of engagement across their sites. In fact, two of the examples discussed, one of strong engagement and one of weak engagement, come from different sites run by the same organization. This may reflect, in part, the challenge of finding and keeping staff with dynamic interpersonal skills.
4. This program also has strong employment retention results, an outcome that may stem, at least in part, from its particularly robust retention services for those who get jobs.

4
Getting Participants Job Ready

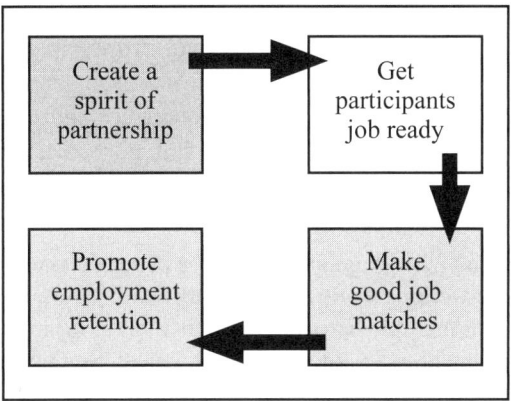

Helping participants become "job ready" is a second common element of work-first employment programs' service strategies. In particular, based on the operations of providers in New York City, programs work with participants to prepare them for job interviews and to discuss potential workplace challenges and employer expectations. They also help people deal with immediately pressing issues that are preventing them from becoming employed, such as housing or child care issues. And finally, programs strive to increase people's motivation to become employed because participants often are apprehensive about leaving welfare for work.

Two types of staff usually take the lead in job-readiness activities. Facilitators, as they are often called, run group workshops on topics such as filling out job applications, interview techniques, succeeding on the job, and transitional benefits. And case managers (or "employment counselors" as they are called at some programs) meet one-on-one with participants to help them deal with barriers to work and prepare them for job interviews.

RATIONALE

Staff at the employment programs characterized program participants into three groups: those who arrive essentially job ready (roughly 10 percent), those who can be helped to become job ready with coaching and assistance (most clients), and long-term recipients (roughly 10 percent) who are hard to employ.

Interviewees said that the share that arrives job ready has fallen since the 1990s because welfare reform has pushed the most employable recipients off of public assistance and into employment. In the words of Karen Smith, the Senior Vice President of Wildcat Industries:[1]

> At this stage of the program, because the people who we could put to work are working, the people now that we're working with are coming with multiple barriers to employment. I mean mental illness, homelessness, long-term unemployment. So this population is very hard to get placed. They're turning down jobs [or] taking the job and not showing up.

Different groups require different types of assistance. The job-ready group simply needs "polishing" and can be sent on job interviews within the first few days. Programs typically focus their energy on the second group. The last group is a challenge, although these individuals can sometimes be placed into jobs with enough effort and coaching.

Barriers to Work

Participants' lack of motivation to leave welfare and begin employment is the most frequently cited barrier to work mentioned by program staff. This is noteworthy, given that personal motivation is rarely mentioned in the literature on barriers to work.[2] "With the population that we deal with . . . they don't have the drive when they first come here," a job developer explained. "They're more comfortable in their predicament. Not that they want to be there—it's just more dependable for them to rely on the system . . . than to depend on themselves to work." Another staff member said, "Motivation and drive is key. Education is important but if you don't have the motivation to get the job, to keep the job, and to do the job that you're supposed to do, then you're not going to be [employed] long."

Staff identified several factors behind some participants' reluctance to become employed, including low self-esteem, a mindset of dependency, fear of the unknown (the workplace), being already employed off the books, and a short-term focus that makes it difficult to see low-wage jobs as stepping stones to higher paying ones in the future. This staff member's comment is representative of many others:

> I'd say the number one barrier is probably psychological . . . Once you've accepted yourself [on welfare], you say, "Ok, now I'm a welfare client." It's very difficult to self-empower back out of that. It also becomes a comfort level for some people . . . who say, "I've got my child care paid for. My rental issues are taken care of for right now." And it's scary to transition back into the world of work.

The fear of doing worse financially by working is an important source of apprehension about leaving welfare. In particular, some participants worry that leaving welfare for work puts them at risk of destitution if they lose their jobs. A program director noted that this concern is particularly acute among long-term recipients:

> People who are habitual welfare recipients—I don't believe are lazy. I believe that it is safer to stay on the rolls of welfare because you know definitely you will have food on the table for your children . . . that you can have medical assistance. But when you sever your ties with that guarantee, there's so much fear. I'm not certain I can feed my child. I'm not certain if my child gets hurt that I can get medical help. So to me it's never laziness. Most often it's fear: Will I be able to provide?

Connected to that fear is the concern among participants that getting back onto welfare could be difficult if they lose their jobs and become unemployed again. A similar concern is that transitional benefits such as Medicaid will be cut off prematurely (in error) once they start working.[3] These fears lead some people to prefer a guaranteed welfare payment over a higher but possibly short-term paycheck. Given the low job-retention rates among welfare recipients in the United States, this preference may be quite rational for some individuals. The realistic tradeoff for many recipients is not between welfare and work, but between welfare and periods of work.

Aside from a lack of motivation, staff mentioned other issues that can hinder employment, including a lack of knowledge about how to apply and interview for jobs, child care issues, attitude problems (aggressiveness, for example), a lack of proper work clothing, unstable housing, and low skills. A workshop facilitator also described the types of family-related issues that can hinder employment:

> Let's say we have a single mother. She's 32 years old. She has five children by five different fathers . . . Every time she goes to work there's something that goes down, she has to leave [work]. I had a young lady, she said . . . "I spent half the night looking for my 13 year old and my 15 year old . . . " She has a job that she has to be at the next morning . . . Will she be able to maintain her job?

A final barrier to work—and especially to staying employed—is a lack of knowledge about workplace norms. Even seemingly simple techniques for navigating the workplace may not come naturally to people who have little work experience. For example, some participants will walk off their jobs when they need to attend to an ill child rather than asking their employers for a day off and are fired as a result.

TECHNIQUES

Several types of staff are involved in job readiness, including orientation staff who begin the process, facilitators who lead job-readiness workshops, and case managers who work with participants one-on-one. Common practices can be divided into three groups. The first group focuses on addressing general barriers to work. The second deals with a specific barrier, the lack of motivation to move from welfare to work. The third group aims to increase the chances that people get hired by making them more marketable to employers.

Addressing Barriers to Work

Every program provides some individual attention to help participants become job ready. Usually this involves meetings between participants and their case managers. The first meeting usually occurs within the first day or two, with successive meetings taking place as needed, from everyday to a few times a week. "What [the case manager] does, which I think is very valuable," a director explained, "is that she really supports the client. She checks over their resume. [She says] 'You can do this. Do you have your clothing? You don't? Ok, we have some.' She really pumps them up . . . and I appreciate that because these folks go get jobs."

Motivating Participants about Employment

Several of the techniques used to help people become job ready have a motivational component that is designed (whether explicitly or implicitly) to boost people's motivation about taking jobs and entering the work world.

Addressing fears about financial loss by leaving welfare

Workers at these employment programs usually explain transitional benefits to participants during workshops. These benefits include Medicaid, Food Stamps, child care subsidies, and the Earned Income Tax Credit. A few sites screen participants to determine which specific benefits they could receive once they start working. And some staff members "do the math" with participants during workshops by explaining how a person's financial situation would improve by working. They may also have broader discussions with people, in groups or one-on-one, about their fears of leaving welfare. "We make a list of all the fears" on the first day, a facilitator explained. "And then we discuss how we can overcome those fears . . . So you address each issue separately . . . That'll help. It doesn't do it the first day [i.e., conquer the fear], but it will help."

Helping people to see entry-level jobs as stepping stones to something better

Staff members often pitch minimum-wage or low-wage jobs as paths to something better. "One of the atrocities I see of welfare," a program director noted, "is the inability to think for yourself and to plan for yourself. Some of them, as simple as that concept appears, think they're going to be stuck in that job forever." If a participant sees a job as a stepping stone, she is more willing to take the job and to "stick it out" once she starts working. Programs therefore emphasize mobility. In the words of one job developer, "Maybe you've been incarcerated for the last 20 years. Who's going to give you a second chance? It's typically going to be a warehouse . . . It doesn't make much to go from 6 to 10 [dollars an hour] in the warehouse field. Then you can grow—you can become a shipping manager. It can go up to be a career. That's how I pitch it to individuals—that you start off here but then you move up."

Emphasizing the benefits of working and being off welfare

Another motivational tool is highlighting the benefits of moving from welfare to work, including nonmonetary benefits.[4] In workshops, some staff members discuss the benefits of being free of the welfare system, with all of its mandates and rules. Others emphasize that working is a more meaningful way to live one's life than reporting to a welfare-to-work program to collect public assistance. "You have to want to do something with your life," one job developer tells participants. "Because if not, someone will make decisions for you. That's why you're here." Still others emphasized the financial benefits of working. Welfare can pay the bills, one staff member explains to participants, but it will never provide enough to travel or to do anything that requires more income.

Building self-esteem

Because participants often have low self-confidence, staff members build the participants' self-esteem, including making people aware of their strengths and positive qualities, to increase their motivation. "You've managed to survive, to put food on the table—that's a strength," a job developer tells participants during orientation. "Let's build on that. Let's build on trying to get you self-reliant, independent, off of HRA [i.e., off welfare]." They also make participants aware that being nervous about starting work is natural. As a job developer said, "The push [giving encouragement] is very important, because it's scary. It's really scary out there when you have to stand on your own two feet when you haven't done it in a while."

Making participants more marketable to employers

All of the programs help people create resumes, secure references, and practice interview techniques. These services are important for a few reasons, as a case manager noted: "A lot of them haven't worked in some time. They've forgotten how to sit in an interview. They've forgotten to do a test run to make sure they get there on time. How to shake hands. How to maintain eye contact. How to present their resume. How to dress . . . They are employable, but we just have to refine their skills a little."

VARIATION IN APPROACHES

Although every program has a job-readiness component, the scope of this activity varies significantly. Some take a more holistic approach to addressing people's work barriers, including focusing on broader life issues such as motivation, self-confidence, and family problems. They also take more time with people (a few weeks to a couple of months) to get them work ready before referring them to job interviews. And some encourage short-term training as a way of making people more marketable.

Other programs take a different approach, focusing more narrowly on issues that affect people's abilities to start work right away, including interview techniques and resume preparation. Staff members at these programs have more urgency about getting people into jobs quickly and less focus on assessing and addressing work barriers.

Another variation among programs (and sometimes among the staff within a particular program) relates to the belief that staff can motivate people to want to leave welfare. The views of staff members can diverge remarkably. Some argue that attending an employment program was not going to change people's mindset, a sentiment expressed by this case manager:

> You try to talk about being independent and "Don't you want to set goals for yourself and be an example?" And they're like "Be an example for what? My mother wasn't on welfare and I haven't taken her example." . . . This is what they've seen or the surroundings they're in. It's just they're so used to it—it's become the norm not to have a nine-to-five per se. So you can't really change the mentality. I've tried.

Others see it as central to their jobs to motivate people to "change their mindset" away from dependency and to "inspire people" to want to live fuller lives by gaining more financial independence.

Notes

1. Only executive-level staff, meaning individuals at senior positions who oversee multiple programs or multiple social service programs, are quoted by name in this study. Program directors, on the other hand, are considered to be staff and given confidentiality.
2. One reason is probably related to research methodology. Motivation is difficult to observe and measure. Another reason may be researchers' reluctance to appear to "blame the victim." As noted earlier, Dunifon and Duncan (1998) examine factors that affect long-term labor-market success, although not among the poor specifically. They found that earnings are strongly affected by an individual's motivation, including their orientation toward challenge and sense of personal control.
3. The latter type of error happens quite regularly, according to a few staff interviewees.
4. Staff opinion was split about whether most people would be immediately better off financially by moving from welfare to work.

5
Making Good Job Matches

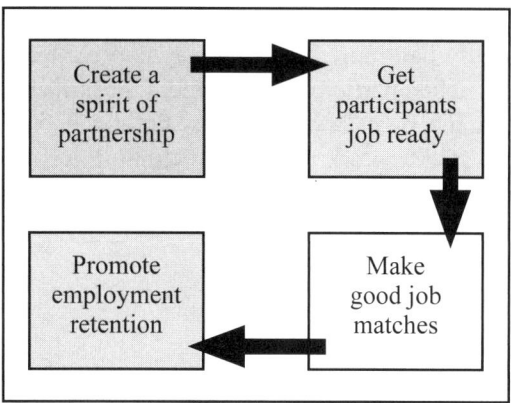

The third common element in New York City's work-first employment program is the focus on making good job matches between participants and employers. That is, once participants are deemed employment ready by the staff, programs attempt to match them with appropriate jobs. Job developers are the central figures in this process, acting as intermediaries between employers and participants. In many cases, employers with existing working relationships with job developers will contact those job developers when they have positions to fill. Some job developers also obtain job leads by contacting employers or by searching want ads. With job leads in hand, they determine which participants are good candidates for particular job openings, often through one-on-one meetings with participants. More rarely, the process is reversed. If participants have more specialized skills or interests, job developers use their contacts to search for jobs for those individuals. Either way, when a potential job match is found, job developers set up job interviews for participants. If the person is not hired, the process continues.

These activities are known among programs as "job matching" or "making good job matches." At a minimum, a good job match occurs when a person is placed into a job that fits with his or her skills and interests. Some staff articulated additional characteristics of good job matches, including that a job is acceptable to the participant in terms of wages, work hours, and location; it is not temporary; there are opportunities for advancement; and there is a decent work environment.

The task of finding job leads (at least during the mid 2000s, a period of modest economic growth) was not a challenge at most programs. Job developers usually had more job openings than participants, although sometimes they lacked participants with the right skills to fill those jobs. Others said that the main constraint was finding enough participants who were motivated to work. The task of finding job leads, no doubt, became more challenging as the economy weakened later in the decade.

RATIONALE

Programs focus on making good job matches for two main reasons. The first is employment retention. People with poor job matches are unlikely to stay for long, either because they will be fired for not having the requisite skills or because they will quit because they dislike their jobs. Susan Melocarro, President of Career and Education Consultants, explained:

> If you're forcing someone into a job that they're not interested in, then they're not going to last on that job. What ends up happening is they fall off the job and then you have to place them again . . . So it's much better to know up front what they're interested in and what they're suited to.

A second rationale for making good matches is that it strengthens relationships with employers. If individuals—either in the interview process or once hired—do not fit with what an employer wants, the employer is less likely to seek out other candidates from that program. This rationale is especially important because employers who are "repeat customers" are an important source of job placements.

TECHNIQUES

All of the programs use job developers, and most of the programs secured the majority of their job placements through these staff. The significant role of job developers is noteworthy since, at least anecdotally, welfare-to-work programs in the United States relied mainly on independent job search prior to national welfare reform in 1996.[1] With independent job search, participants take the lead in finding their own jobs. Staff at several programs said that independent job search is not used because it is too easily abused. For example, people can fake their independent job search by collecting business cards to show the staff, while not actually looking for work. As a result, most programs now rely on job developers to find job leads for participants. A few programs supplement the work of job developers by encouraging participants to find leads as well. One organization, for example, offers $50 to participants who become employed in positions that they find themselves. About a quarter of placements at this program are self-directed, staff said.

One program uses a "guided job search" approach. Under this approach, the staff teaches participants how to find jobs (similar to independent job search) but closely supervises the process. Judging from limited evidence—participants' outcomes at this one program—it does not appear that guided job search is an effective strategy. The program had the third-lowest job-placement rate among the 26 programs, and fewer participants than average become employed for at least six months. Appendix B describes guided job search in more detail.

Given the central role of job developers at most programs, the rest of the chapter focuses on how they conduct job matching. The matching process is about screening—job developers screen participants for employers while also screening employers for participants.

Screening and Assisting Participants

Guiding people toward good job matches

To make job matches, job developers talk with participants and learn about their strengths, limitations, skills, and interests. Participants often have ideas about what types of jobs they would like to aim for. Job developers, in turn, give guidance about which types of jobs are most in demand by employers, and they sometimes encourage participants to consider fields they have not have considered before. Job developers also help people understand the types of jobs and wages they can realistically obtain. As one explained, "They sometimes need to come back to reality because sometimes they may be stay-at-home mothers who haven't been to work in 10 years and they think they're clerical and have computer skills . . . It's a big reality check."

Preparing participants for interviews

Although workshop facilitators and case managers usually play the lead role in providing interview preparation, some job developers participate as well by conducting mock interviews. Since job developers usually know which skills and qualities particular employers are looking for, they can coach participants to emphasize those aspects. Mock interviews also help job developers check whether people are adequately prepared for their interviews, something that is important to protect job developers' relationships with employers.

Building Relationships with Employers

Understanding and meeting employers' needs

Job developers try to build relationships with employers and learn their staffing needs, although the time actually devoted to relationship building varies. For example, some job developers communicate with employers mainly by phone. Others spend a portion of each week in the field, meeting with employers in person, as described by this job developer:

> You have to be able to go out into the field and network with people and get to know what they're looking for when they hire someone . . . Get an idea of the skills they need. If someone tells me they need someone to do Excel, is it basic, intermediate, or advanced? How many words per minute typing? Talk to me about the chemistry [office culture]. Is it fast paced or a little laid back? It's very important that you get as close of a match as possible . . . If I don't send the right person to that position, [the employer] is gone—they're history.

Good job matches are the foundation for a potentially symbiotic relationship between job developers and employers. If these staff carefully screen participants for employers, those employers will, hopefully, contact the program the next time it needs more workers.

Offering "human resources" services to firms

A few job developers try to solidify their relationships with employers by offering to act as auxiliary human resources staff for firms, particularly in dealing with participants who are having trouble on the job. If an individual starts showing up late for work, for example, the employer can call the job developer and ask him or her to speak with the person and, hopefully, avoid firing the employee. The offer of HR services could be part of some programs' employment-retention strategies, but in practice, it appears to be mainly a marketing strategy by programs to engage employers. Job developers said that it was rare that employers actually called them for help in dealing with problem employees.

Screening employers

Another reason some job developers spend time in the field is to determine which workplaces have favorable environments for participants. For example, one job developer said that he looks to see if employees seem happy when he visits firms. If so, "I pitch that to my candidates [the participants]." He added: "I deal with the union shop ones that . . . make you feel like you're achieving something and they give you raises as time goes on. You get treated better." A director at another program explained that, because most of the potential milestone payments (programs' performance-based compensation) are based on retention, her program is "more conscientious about the partnerships we form" with employers. "People don't stay in their jobs to get us paid," she noted. "They stay in their jobs because it pays enough, they like what they're doing, they feel appreciated in what they're doing, and they're going to meet the demands of their family life through their work."

VARIATION IN APPROACHES

Staff at most programs articulated the importance of making good job matches, and none of the interviewees said that job matching was unimportant. But some program leaders place more pressure on staff to make placements and are willing to sacrifice the quality of job matches to make their placement goals. For example, a job developer at a small faith-based nonprofit felt overworked and often had to focus on getting people out the door, not on making careful job matches. "If I had another job developer," she said, "it would give me more time to work with this person—not just send them into any job just to get the placement. Because remember, I also have to think about the placement. If we don't make the placement, our agency will be lost [financially]."[2] At another nonprofit, a site director felt considerable pressure (and exerted it on his staff) to meet monthly placement goals set by the organization's leadership. Meeting those goals sometimes means encouraging people to take any available job, as he explained:

> Retention is where the money is, so we want to push for making the right match . . . But a lot of times, if we're in a crunch and we need to make a push, we will make an extra effort to just get people out there, because a job is better than no job and if they're making six, seven dollars an hour, they're making more than they are on [public] assistance . . . Ideally we'd want to invest a lot of time in them and then allow them to really explore what their real interest is. But the truth of the matter is I don't have past the end of the month [to make my monthly goals]. If I have to make my numbers, I have to get you out there.[3]

Other programs, meanwhile, have a strong ethic about not pushing anyone into a job just to make placement goals even though all of the programs had monthly placement goals for their programs as a whole or, in some cases, for each of their job developers. Staff at these programs talked about being focused on people's well-being and not being "numbers focused." In fact, some programs were willing to have a greater emphasis on case management even if it meant losing money on the contract with the city. A director at another small faith-based nonprofit explained, "We do have a [placement] goal and we talk about the goal, but we do not take matching a person to a job that is not desirable for them over 'we need to get this placement no matter what.'" Her staff articulated a similar philosophy.

This small faith-based nonprofit (call it Site A) and the previously discussed one (Site B) where the site director felt strong pressure to get people into jobs represent different ends of the spectrum in terms of their emphasis on job matching. Both aim to make good matches, but for Site B, reaching its numeric placement goals is the top priority. Do these differences affect their performance? Figure 5.1 shows a comparison of job placement and employment retention data for both sites.[4] Consistent with expectations, Site B has a significantly higher overall placement rate, but Site A has a larger share of people placed in high-wage jobs, using HRA's definition of high wage.[5] Surprisingly, the share of placed participants that is still working six months later is fairly similar at both programs. The fourth set of columns in Figure 5.1 shows the best available measure of overall performance: the six-month caseload employment rate, meaning the share of all participants (not just those placed in jobs) that becomes employed and is still working at any job six months later. The results show substantially better outcomes at Site B (11 percent) than Site A (7 percent). Of course, neither of these results is an uplifting level of success, underscoring the challenge of helping welfare recipients get and keep jobs. But Site B's performance on this measure is nonetheless more than 50 percent better than Site A's.

Figure 5.1 Commitment to Job Matching: An Example of Two Programs

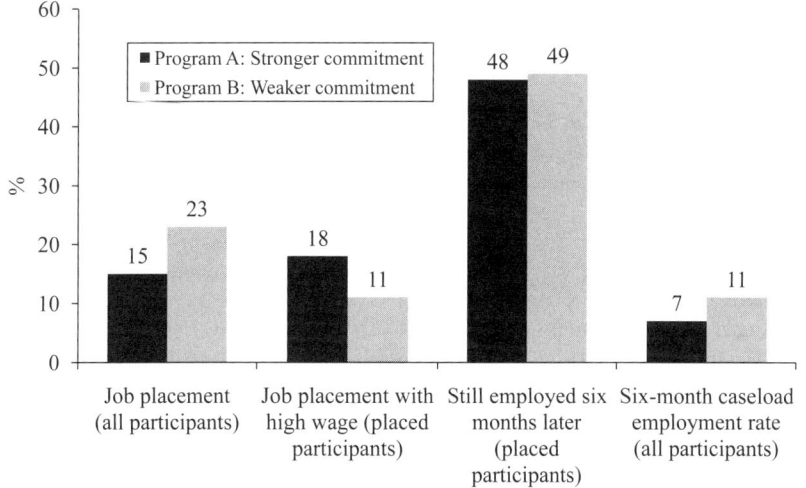

58 Feldman

These results imply that, although the quality of job matching may be important for promoting sustained employment, it is only one aspect that can affect employment retention. For example, Site A is more careful in its job matching and aimed for higher quality jobs, but it lacks any retention staff. Site B is focused on quick placement, but it has a retention staff to help people stay employed.

A final aspect of variation in terms of job matching relates to pay. Only one organization, a for-profit provider, ties the pay of its job developers to the employment-retention of participants that they place into jobs.[6] At the two sites run by this firm, the majority of job developers' potential pay is tied to the number of people they place that achieve the three- and six-month employment-retention milestones. An executive explained that under their compensation plan for job developers, "you don't get a lot for the placement; you get a few dollars. But you get money on the back end for retention. You give me quality jobs where people stay and the big payoff is there . . . It mirrors the goals of the contract [with the city]."[7] Surprisingly, however, employment-retention outcomes at these two sites are not particularly strong. The share of placed participants who are still working six months later at these programs (46 percent and 44 percent, respectively) is near the average of the other programs in New York City (45 percent).

Based on this limited evidence, at least, it appears that retention incentives for job developers are not enough, in themselves, to substantially affect performance.

Notes

1. Even today, independent job search is the predominant type of job-search assistance under the WIA. It is difficult, however, to apply any lessons from welfare-to-work programs under TANF (such as those in New York City) to employment services under WIA because TANF and WIA target different populations. Recall that WIA services are voluntary and are not geared to those on public assistance.
2. Interestingly, there was no clear connection between the number of job developers at a program (relative to the number of participants served) and placement rates. The correlation (−0.28) is relatively small, negative, and not statistically significant (P = 0.19). So too is the correlation (−0.15, P = 0.48) when outcomes are defined as six-month employment retention rates among placed participants. In short, while job developers play a central role in these programs—obtaining most of the job leads for participants—differences in job-development staff capacity do not appear to drive differences in program performance.
3. He explained that to give people a push, "we'll say 'Take this job now, because that job may lead to a better job.' Or 'Take this part-time job now, and you will

continue coming to us for the remaining hours and we'll help you get a second part-time job, or another full-time job.'"

4. These results are for participants, defined in this study as those assigned to employment programs who showed up for at least a day.
5. HRA defines "high wage" jobs as those paying at least $344 per week.
6. Other programs pay job developers straight salaries, or salaries plus bonuses tied to placement, but not retention. Moreover, aside from pay, many sites set monthly placement (not retention) quotas for job developers.
7. Why don't more programs use retention incentives for job developers? Some programs may see holding job developers accountable for retention as unfair. As Karen Smith of Wildcat Industries, noted: "We did it [had incentive pay for job developers based on retention] for a little while, but it didn't make sense because the job developers have really no control over that—it's really the case managers." People often lose their jobs, she said, because of an inability to cope with problems: "They're going to have an issue and instead of dealing with that issue they're going to walk away [from their jobs]." According her view, in other words, the quality of job matching has little effect on retention rates.

6
Promoting Employment Retention

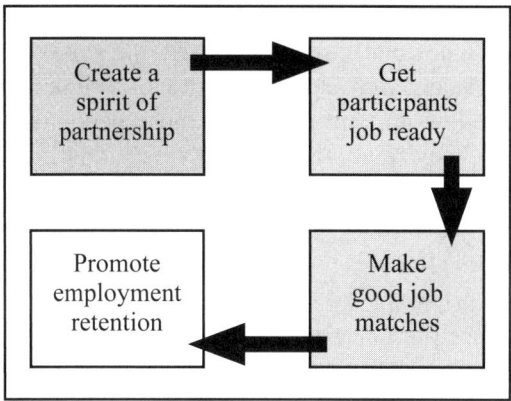

Providing postplacement services to help people stay working once they become employed is the fourth and final common element among today's work-first programs in New York City. These services typically involve keeping in touch with participants to offer support and encouragement, and helping people find new jobs if they become unemployed again. Some programs have retention specialists who work solely on these issues, whereas others use case managers to provide retention assistance.

RATIONALE

Many welfare recipients in the United States lose their jobs within the first few months of employment. In particular, studies from the mid 1990s showed that about one-fourth of recipients who became employed stopped working within three months and at least half were no longer working within one year (Strawn and Martinson 2000). At one well-known program, Project Match in Chicago, 55 percent of participants lost or quit their job within six months and 71 percent did so within a year (Wagner et al. 1998). The results from New York City, from the mid 2000s, illustrate that employment retention remains a critical challenge. More than a third (37 percent) of program participants placed into jobs were jobless again three months later, and more than half (56 percent) were jobless within six months.

To help people stay employed, New York City's welfare-to-work programs provide postplacement services. In the words of Karen Smith, Senior Vice President of Wildcat Industries, "Without intensive case management, follow-up, and prodding, those people are not going to stay on the job. They're going to have an issue and instead of dealing with that issue they're going to walk away." Peter Cove, the founder of America Works, elaborated on the reasons behind many participants' short employment spans:

> We believe that people lose their jobs . . . because they don't fit in the workplace [including] the mores of the workplace. What do you do when you don't have anything to do? How do you handle authority? And also the things that happen on the outside [of work]: The sick child, the day care that falls out, the bad transportation, the housing, the abusive mate—the things that many of us [who are not poor] have supports for and ways of dealing with. We have resources. The people we're dealing with often do not.

Staff cited other factors such as low work hours that can cause people to quit out of frustration or they were given jobs that turned out to be temporary.

TECHNIQUES

Retention practices can be grouped into two categories: monitoring participants' employment progress and providing reemployment services.

Monitoring Working Participants' Progress

Encouraging participants who become employed to stay in touch

To encourage contact between working participants and program staff, programs offer subway passes, paid for by the city. The passes are available for up to six months after starting work. To receive them, individuals must bring in their pay stubs to their program office every two weeks to prove they are still working. (Staff said that about half of working participants come in to pick them up.) This gives staff members an opportunity to provide encouragement and to ask people about their progress on the job. A retention counselor described a typical interchange: "I do small talk: 'How's work? Is your child care in place? Are you getting your Food Stamps, Medicaid?'"[1]

Keeping in touch with working participants by phone

Many programs contact working participants by phone, although the frequency of contact varies. Some make calls a few weeks before the three- and six-month retention milestone dates. If a staff member learns that a participant is no longer working, the participant is encouraged to return to the program to be placed in a new job so that the program can get compensated for retention milestones. Other providers check in by phone every few weeks, including some that have evening call shifts to reach people after work.

In terms of the effect of these calls on employment retention, some staff said that their advice and encouragement helps prevent participants' job losses. Others felt that the main benefit of phone contact is to find out if people had lost jobs, so they can get them reemployed faster. "We don't really save them from losing the job," one staff member noted, "but we help them out more quickly."

Contacting working participants during the first week of employment

Some programs check in with participants by phone a few days after job placement. Others encourage participants to contact the staff, especially during the first week of employment, if they need help or advice. "That first week becomes crucial," a job developer explained. "I say, 'If you feel stressed, that first week is going to be [a challenge]. But stick it out. Call me.' Once they get through that first week, that second week, things start to fall into place. They start to feel better."

Providing Reemployment and Job-Upgrading Assistance

Finding new jobs for people who become unemployed again

When a program learns that a participant has lost a job, it encourages that person to come back to the program to receive help in finding a new job. A few job developers said they needed to find some people as many as three different jobs within six months to keep them working. "A large percentage of our people we place more than once," said Lee Bowles, CEO of America Works. They do this "in part to upgrade and in part to find the right match."

Helping employed participants change jobs

Many providers emphasize that they will help participants change jobs if they are dissatisfied with their current ones or if they want to get higher paying jobs. At the same time, though, they also encourage people to "stick it out" in their current jobs to get more work experience. "If it really gets to the point where they're feeling like they've got to quit," a retention counselor explained, "I'll tell them don't quit. Come in first to find another job." The actual amount of help participants receive to change or upgrade their jobs is unclear. One manager noted that getting staff to provide that type of service to working individuals is not easy, given the large number of people they serve and the fact that job developers often think that "their job is done" once someone gets placed.

VARIATION IN APPROACHES

Employment retention efforts vary considerably. Some sites focus mainly on obtaining verifications—proof that people are working so that the program can get paid for those milestones—whereas others provide more intensive follow-up and assistance. These different approaches are illustrated by a program that had recently shifted from a less-intensive approach to retention services to a more-intensive one. Prior to the change, case managers were in charge of verification and retention, but in practice, they had little time to do either. A new retention unit was created with three full-time retention counselors, and its task was contacting participants every two weeks. A job developer from this program explained:

> Now they're actually managing the case as opposed to calling to make sure you're still at the company. When case managers were doing retention, they were basically just collecting pay stubs . . . [Now] they've become your postplacement manager and they'll call you up: "I know you're working at this place for a while. Are you ok? Is there anything we can do to help you?" [The participant may say:] "Yeah, I have a problem with my child care," or "Yeah, HRA called me for a meeting, but I have to work, so what do I do?"

This site has one of the highest ratios of retention staff per capita and is also a top performer in terms of retention. It has the highest rate (74 percent) of placed participants still working after three months, and the second-highest rate (56 percent) after six months.[2] On the other hand, other programs that provide robust retention services had more modest results. Across all the 26 programs in New York City, in fact, there is no statistically significant correlation between the number of retention staff per participant and retention outcomes.[3] This result underscores a theme in the welfare-to-work literature of the difficulty in finding effective practices for promoting job retention.

The way staff members track retention-related data also varied. For example, a few programs have customized computer systems that allow staff to track the number of contacts with each working participant, their retention milestone dates, and more. Others use pen and paper lists. Moreover, some program directors monitor staff in terms of the frequency of retention follow up, while others are more informal. Yet no simple connection apparently exists between program performance and these tracking or management factors. The program with the most sophisticated computer tracking system and close monitoring by management of employment retention issues had only average retention outcomes.

Finally, in terms of variation, at least one program, a small faith-based nonprofit, has an explicit strategy of calling participants a week before their retention milestone dates and, if they are unemployed, attempting to quickly place them into new jobs. The staff calls this approach "rapid reattachment." The results show only average employment-retention rates at the three-month mark, but the highest rates at six months, suggesting that this practice may boost performance as measured by milestone achievement. Of course, this strategy could also be viewed as gaming the contract, since this program's retention focus is on getting people reemployed just prior to the contractual milestone dates on which programs get paid if people are working. The staff said that this was simply doing what the contract wanted: placing people in jobs and following-up to help them get new jobs if they were unemployed again.

Notes

1. Programs also use wage stubs to document their retention milestones so they can be compensated by the city under their pay-for-performance contracts.
2. Other factors at this program may have contributed to this program's strong retention results. This is the same site that discouraged unmotivated participants from staying in the program during the first few days and, likely as a result, had high dropout rates.
3. The correlation at the six-month mark was 0.12 ($P = 0.57$). The correlation at the three-month mark was actually slightly negative.

Part 2

Differences in Organizational Practices among Work-First Employment Programs

7
Different Practices among Programs

Although work-first employment programs share several common elements, important differences exist as well. This chapter explores four of the most evident differences among welfare-to-work programs in New York City. These differences include the extent to which programs emphasize a quick-placement versus a case-management approach, encourage short-term job training prior to job search versus immediate job search, deem participants employable, and refer participants to sanctioning for noncompliance. As we will see later in this volume, some of these operational differences help explain why certain programs have better employment outcomes than others.

QUICK PLACEMENT VERSUS CASE MANAGEMENT

A "quick-placement approach" means something different today than it did in the past. Relative to programs that operated before national welfare reform in 1996—and before a work-first approach became ubiquitous—every one of the 26 welfare-to-work programs in New York City would be considered quick-placement focused. In other words, all of the programs have employment as the goal and all of them aim to move participants into work within a few weeks or a couple of months. Yet within today's work-first framework, there is still considerable variation in placement speeds among programs. The variation stems from the fact that some programs have a stronger emphasis on getting people into jobs quickly (referred to here as a quick-placement approach), whereas others have a stronger emphasis on providing job-readiness assistance (a case-management approach).

Figure 7.1 shows the median number of days it takes each program to place participants (among those who became employed) into jobs.[1] At the fastest site, half of all participants who became employed do so within 35 days. At the slowest site, this occurs within 84 days, almost two-and-a-half times as long as at the fastest one. The average among programs is 56 days. Not surprisingly, programs that place people into jobs faster have more urgency about making placements. At some programs, in fact, a significant portion of individuals goes on job interviews within a few days. To speed up the placement process, quick-placement programs spend less time on case management. The figure also shows that most of the programs that use job training (defined as sending at least 5 percent of participants to training) are at the slow end of placement speeds.

One might conjecture that placement speeds are not only a function of urgency among program staff, but also a function of staffing capacity. In other words, having a larger staff (relative to the number of participants) could speed up job-readiness activities and job matching. But the data show, however, that placement speeds are not a function of staff-to-participant ratios, whether defined in terms of specific types of staff or the staff as a whole. Instead, a focus on quick placement—and a de-emphasis of case management—appears to be the main driver of

Figure 7.1 Median Number of Days between Program Entry and Job Start Date, among Those Who Become Employed

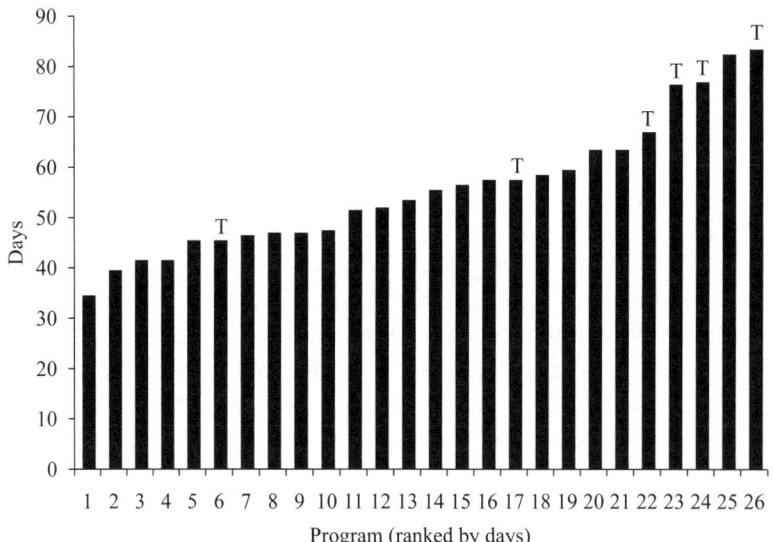

NOTE: T = program uses job training.

placement speeds. What program staff members do appears to matter more than how many of them do it.

The Rationale for Quick Placement

The rationale for having more urgency about getting people into jobs comes, in part, from a belief that welfare recipients can often fix their own barriers to work, or at least work around them, once they become employed. To illustrate this point, Peter Cove, founder of America Works, provided an example of a hypothetical participant, Shirley, who fixes her lack of child care. New York City pays for child care for welfare recipients with young children, so this example presumably deals with someone with school-aged children.

> Barnes & Noble says, "Shirley, can you come in next Monday for training to be a cashier?" What do you know, the next day Shirley found an aunt that can take care of the kid, or she found a local day care provider. What was going on before was insecurity about going to work—that she'd been paid for a long time not to go to work [so she used to say] "I don't have any day care to take care of my kids." All of a sudden somebody wants Shirley. Shirley's like, "Wow, wait a second. Maybe I can find somebody to take care of my kids."[2]

Another rationale for quick placement is that a sense of urgency about getting people into jobs is the most motivating to participants. "We have motivational workshops," a program director noted, "but the one motivation that best works for us is real job leads." A job developer also explained how participants were wary when they heard that they would be going on job interviews within a few days. "Then all of a sudden," she said, "I'm sending people out [on interviews]. And by Friday there'll be [only] five people sitting here because we have them all out and hopefully working. So they start realizing we're serious." Another job developer added, "You have to earn their respect . . . When they start meeting our companies [i.e., employers], when they finally get an interview, not just some [workshop] nonsense, that alone makes them feel better."

A third reason for emphasizing quick placement is that the job-search process is a useful way to elicit information about people's employability—a more effective way, according to proponents, than assessments by case managers. In the words of Peter Cove:

> We said the job is the important thing, and we can't make an assumption about which of the things [barriers] is going to blow them out of the water. We don't know . . . So what we're going to do is to provide them a path to let them move toward the job, but we're going to stay on top of them very carefully so if something comes up that gets in the way, that's when we intervene.

In particular, some participants appear to be work ready until they face the actual prospect of a job interview, and they call in sick or say they do not have child care. "You start to realize that, although they want to work, they're afraid," a case manager explained. "They're not as job ready as they seem." At the same time, some people who initially do not appear job ready can do fine once they start working. "Many times clients that you believe don't have the motivation may end up actually getting a job and doing well," noted a job developer. "If they have a fear [of starting work] and if they actually overcome that fear working on the job . . . it changes them."

A final rationale for quick placement articulated by some program leaders is that, according to them, it is the only financially viable approach under New York City's pay-for-performance contracts. While more "hand holding" might be helpful for some participants, more personalized case management is too expensive to provide. This rationale is not limited to for-profit providers. A director of one nonprofit, for example, said that he would be willing to allow his case managers to provide more individualized help "if we got paid for it." He instructs his staff to focus on getting people jobs, not on social work.

Program Practices within a Quick-Placement Approach

Programs create a sense of urgency about getting people into jobs in several ways. One is by setting expectations, during orientation, about quickly placing participants into jobs, explaining that work is the goal, jobs are available, and people will be sent on interviews as soon as they are deemed job ready—likely a matter of days or a couple of weeks. Job training is typically not encouraged.

Participants at quick-placement sites usually meet with job developers during the first day or two of the program to begin preparing for job interviews or, for those who are already job ready, to be sent on interviews. Job developers at these programs have an obvious focus on speed. "Part of why I've been successful here is that I work with a sense of urgency," one said. "I want to get you working as soon as possible. I don't need to talk to you 10 times before I can figure out where I need to place you."

Case managers, meanwhile, reinforce a sense of urgency in one-on-one meetings by focusing on vocational issues rather than broader life issues. These vocational issues include practicing for job interviews and dealing with immediately pressing barriers to work such as having the appropriate work clothes and ensuring that child care arrangements have been made. The message from case managers, a staff member explained, is: "I've got two weeks to hold your hand and then I'm going to let you go. Tell me what I need to do for you and we will do this. Just know that by the end of two weeks, you need to have gotten yourself together." She said that participants often prefer case managers who do not apply that type of pressure because "they think that person is helping them [by being more lenient], but you're really not."

Interestingly, one for-profit provider with relatively quick placement speed has no case managers at all. There is a social worker available if people need special assistance, but meeting with him is not mandatory. A program leader explained the rationale, "If they have a problem, they get referred to someone here [the social worker] to try to help them with that problem. But we don't assume there's a problem. When you assume there's a problem, you're going to find it, because that will be someone's job."

Looking across programs, though, there is essentially no correlation between placement speed and the number of case managers per participant.[3] Some quick-placement programs actually have robust case-management staffs, including one that has the second-highest case-management capacity. A robust case-management staff, in other words, does not preclude a program from creating urgency about placement. The focus of case managers and the messages they convey to participants are more important than how many case managers there are.

Job-readiness workshops at quick-placement programs last for a week or two—somewhat shorter, on average, than those at case-management-focused programs. Moreover, staff at some quick-placement providers noted that they send people on job interviews as soon as they are ready, rather than waiting until they complete the workshops.

An interesting perspective on these issues comes from a site director who was hired to restructure a program to emphasize quicker placements. Before he was hired, job-readiness workshops were two weeks long and participants only met with job developers after the workshops were completed. "That changed," he said. "I cut down the workshops to a week. And those who can be fast tracked see their job developer right away . . . The job developers introduce themselves during the second day of orientation. They are sharing job leads and people are going out [on interviews] that day."

To encourage a sense of urgency among the staff, a few quick-placement programs give their job developers financial bonuses for meeting placement goals. And managers at most programs, whether quick-placement or case-management focused, set monthly placement goals for job developers. But quick-placement sites were more likely to have office-wide placement or revenue goals as well, not just individual goals for job developers. "Every week we try to have a meeting to discuss the billing, the placements, how it's going," a case manager at a nonprofit explained. "It sort of gives us a little push, since we know we have to meet our goal of $125,000 a month." At another quick-placement site, a faith-based one, the director holds a staff meeting each week "so the staff knows where we are goal-wise for the month," he said. "They know what our operating cost is, monthly. It has to be real for them. If it's just these numbers and there's no dollar figures attached to it, to them it means nothing."[4]

Another distinction is that staff at quick-placement programs are more likely to view their organizations as both social service agencies and businesses, while staff at programs with a case-management approach see themselves more solidly in the social service field. Leaders at quick-placement sites also place more emphasis on covering program costs. "This agency is a nonprofit but I'm supposed to have a balanced bottom line or else we don't stay operating," explained Linda Stewart, Senior Vice President of Goodwill Industries of New York and Northern New Jersey, which operates three of the welfare-to-work sites. "That trickles down to staff . . . We are very much run like a business compared to a lot of nonprofits. I get monthly revenue and expense reports for every single program and detailed budget sheets from everything we purchase."

The Rationale for Case Management

Rather than emphasizing speed in placing people into jobs, work-first providers with a case-management approach emphasize job readiness. The main rationale for providing more job-readiness assistance is that, according to proponents, people will stay employed longer if their barriers are addressed before they begin working. Anyone can be "pushed" into a job, a staff member explained, but that rarely leads to sustained employment. By working with people more intensively before employment, and by allowing them more time to get their lives in order, these programs aim to increase participants' employment retention. This type of assistance can take weeks, if not months, as this director of a case-management-focused site explained:

> If they were ready for work they would not be here. They [the city welfare department] are sending these individuals to us because they are difficult to place or else they would have been placed already. So I see if these people [can become employed] with a little bit of understanding, a little bit of coaxing . . . We need to keep them a little longer because we see a person who [for example] is very introverted. It takes a month to warm up. They start talking. They start looking you in the eyes.

The need to address barriers is especially important today, some staff noted, because the welfare caseload has gotten more disadvantaged over time. A program director explained the implications:

> You can't operate the way we did in 1999 because we're operating with people that, first of all, really don't want to work. But HRA is mandating, "You have to go do work." We need to say to them, "Alright, let's change this whole mindset here." Changing a mindset is not done overnight, especially for someone that's come with a strong resistance that "I'm not going to work. I've made it so far on public assistance for 10 or 15 years."

The view among these programs that job-readiness is the first issue that needs to be addressed, prior to job search, contrasts with the view among quick-placement programs, where employment is the first priority. Each approach, in other words, has a different conceptual model of the most effective path to self-sufficiency (see Figure 7.2). Of course, all of the programs provide some upfront help to address work barriers and job readiness, so the difference between these approaches is a matter of service intensity. Moreover, neither set of programs naïvely believes that their approach produces a direct route to self-sufficiency for most participants, given the high rate of job loss among those placed in jobs. But each side believes that their approach puts people on a faster track towards sustained employment and self-sufficiency.

Another rationale for the case-management approach is that, according to proponents, taking time to help people with their problems builds stronger relationships with staff. Stronger relationships, in turn, make it more likely that people will stay in contact with the program after placement. That contact allows staff to assist participants who are having difficulties in their jobs or have lost their jobs. "The retention rates are much better if you address the big issues [in people's lives] because they'll always come back to you like you're their mentor, their friend, their psychotherapist," a case manager explained.

Staff members at programs with a case-management approach have mixed opinions about whether more intensive job-readiness assistance also increases placement rates, as opposed to employment-retention rates. Some felt that it does. As a job developer noted, there can be job leads available, "but if the clients aren't ready—don't do well on interviews, don't have their resumes ready, don't have the right attire, don't have the right attitude—they're not going to get the job." On the other

Figure 7.2 Two Models of Moving to Self-Sufficiency

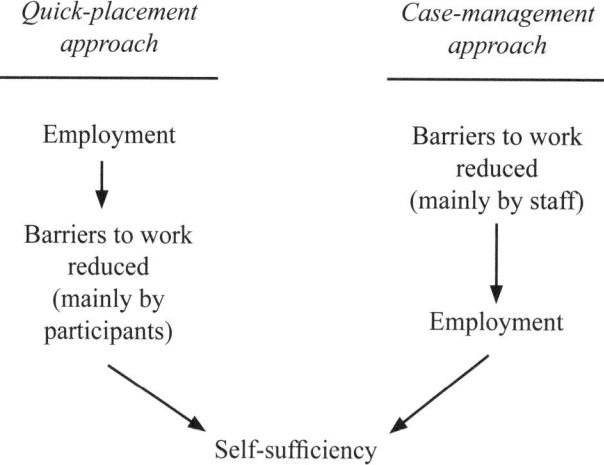

hand, a director at a program with a case-management approach predicted that if they provided less individual attention they would make more placements, but their employment retention rates would suffer.

Program Practices within a Case-Management Approach

Providers with a case-management focus take a more holistic approach to addressing people's problems, rather than focusing only on immediate job-preparation issues. More time is spent on work readiness through one-on-one meetings and in workshops. Moreover, job developers at these sites are more willing to spend time finding people jobs that have better pay or are better matched with people's interests. Some programs, for example, try to avoid placing any participants in minimum-wage jobs. This contrasts with the view at quick-placement programs, where staff members tend to see minimum-wage jobs as useful starting points for people with low skills.

Programs with a case-management approach are also less focused on performance measures than their quick-placement counterparts. In fact, staff members tend to characterize their programs as purposefully not "numbers" focused. A director at a nonprofit that emphasized job-readiness assistance, for example, characterized her program as more "help driven" than "number driven." She said her program has monthly placement targets, but she was unsure exactly what they were. Too much of a focus on placement targets, she noted, can lead staff to push people into taking jobs that are not a good fit for them.

SHORT-TERM JOB TRAINING VERSUS IMMEDIATE JOB SEARCH

Another key difference among programs is that some encourage participants to enroll in short-term, classroom-based job training prior to job search, while others discourage training altogether.[5] Even for the most training-friendly programs, though, the message is not that training is always a better option than direct job placement. Instead, the message is that training may be a useful option for some participants. "Everyone [in the welfare system] is telling them what to do," a director explained. "No one is listening and saying 'What would you like to do?' ... So we let them choose what they want to do—either to go to work or to go to training. Most of the clients choose training because they know they're lacking the skills to be able to become employable in the marketplace." The training programs used by these programs run for up to six months, the maximum allowed by New York City. But courses generally last just one or two months or less—much shorter than the typical training programs of a few decades ago, reflecting the shift towards work first.

Most programs that encourage training refer participants to outside, private training providers, but some run training courses themselves. Figure 7.3 shows the percentage of participants at each site that receive training vouchers. The $1,500 vouchers are paid for by the city and allow qualified participants to attend one of hundreds of city-approved training programs. These include training in customer service, carpentry, and office-computer skills. Most voucher-eligible training courses are geared towards the more advantaged participants in the caseload who have strong basic skills and, often, a high school degree. As the figure shows, half of the sites refer participants to training, with the percentage ranging from 1 to 16 percent of their caseloads.

Figure 7.3 Percentage of Participants That Receive Training Vouchers

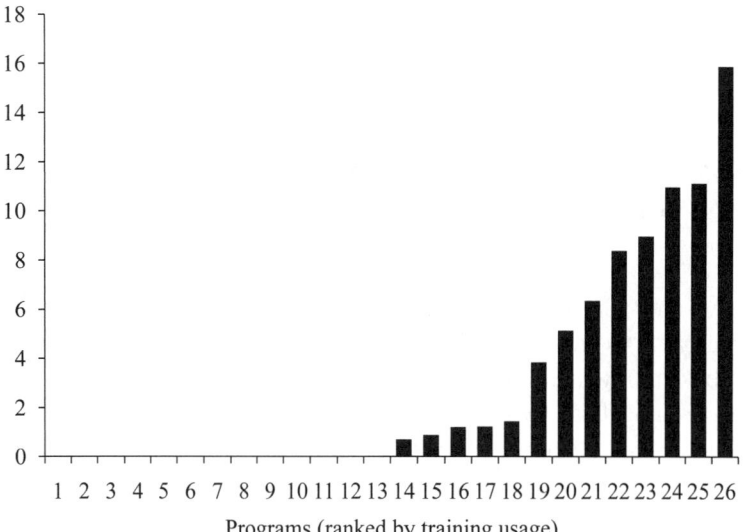

Programs (ranked by training usage)

Programs also refer participants to short-term free training provided by employers or employer associations. These courses include training to be a home health aid, security guard, or food service worker. They typically last between a week and six weeks and are more accessible to participants with lower skills compared to voucher-eligible courses. System-wide data on the usage of these free courses are not available, but fieldwork shows that programs that send a higher proportion of participants to voucher training also send more participants to free employer-sponsored training.

The Rationale for Job Training

Programs that encourage short-term training do so for three main reasons. The first, according to proponents, is that it helps motivate people to want to work because it allows them to obtain higher paying jobs. "That's why training is so valuable," a program director explained. "If you're making . . . $11.75 an hour, or certainly $15, $16, now we're talking about a paycheck. They can see a possible light at the end of the tunnel. They can see a career track."[6] A second rationale is to make people more marketable. "A lot of times [programs] send people out on interviews, but they're not focused on what is going to make that person more marketable if their skills are not up to par," explained a case manager at a program that runs several training programs itself. "If they're going for a clerical or customer service job, they need to know basic computer [skills]." Some staff said that training is especially beneficial for those who have not worked recently or who are having trouble being placed in a job. "If they've been sent out on interviews and they don't land [any jobs], then there's a good possibility they need to upgrade their skills," a staff member said. "We put them in training and send them back out again. Give them a brush up course." And finally, a third rationale is that it leads to better employment retention. In particular, training can lead to higher paying jobs that tend to be more stable. And participants may make more of an effort to keep higher paying jobs.

Proponents also argue that having training as an option is useful because, as Career and Education Consultants owner Susan Melocarro explained, one size does not fit all: "Some people need training and want it. Other people just want to go to work. I think you're force fitting if you try to send everybody out for direct placement and don't offer training."

Common Approaches to Job Training

Programs that encourage training often develop close relationships with training providers. A few programs, in fact, have training providers co-located with them at their sites. Alternatively, a handful of programs operate their own training courses and are therefore able to collect training voucher payments themselves. Programs that encourage training often have training providers give presentations to participants during orientation to describe their training courses and placement results. If a participant expresses an interest in job training, staff members screen them to see if they are good candidates. Because some participants use training to avoid work requirements or to try to continue working off the books, the staff must investigate if there is a legitimate need for training. To do that, they determine whether participants' skill levels match the training course requirements, ask participants about their employment goals, and examine their attendance records at past employment programs via computerized case histories. They also examine current attendance, since eligibility for a training voucher requires at least a month of excellent attendance at their current employment program.[7]

If the staff agrees that training is a useful option, they suggest training providers that they know have good placement results to participants. This knowledge is based on their experience, rather than data, since New York City does not track training outcomes. If the training program is voucher eligible, the staff applies for an HRA voucher. To be approved, individuals must show that they have considered a few different training providers, so staff members typically ask participants to do site visits at several providers.

While participants attend training, the staff monitors their attendance, as required by the city, by getting weekly attendance reports from the training providers. Some staff members ask trainers to contact them right away if someone starts skipping classes so they can intervene quickly to investigate why the person is truant and to let them know that they risk sanctioning if they continue to be absent without cause.

Most programs that encourage training view it as something that precedes job search, but a few programs encourage training only after someone has been unsuccessful in their job search. This approach can mesh training with a quick-placement focus. Programs create a sense of urgency about direct placement but discuss training options with those who are not placed within a few weeks.

Some programs discourage any type of training before placement, but they offer to help people find evening classes once they become employed. The staff at these programs noted, however, that once people start working, interest in training usually wanes, either because training seems less necessary or because of a lack of time. As a result, few people actually take this employment-then-training route.

Staff at programs that encourage training said the effort they expend to evaluate trainers and participants, and to monitor participants during training, is worth it. Some programs, for example, credit the majority of their job placements to training programs. And some reduce staffing costs by relying on trainers to make some or most of their job placements. As a director explained, "We only deal with voucher schools [i.e., training providers] that do job placement. If vouchers weren't in the mix, you might hear me sing a different tune [about needing more job developers on staff]." Moreover, the handful of programs that operate their own training programs can control the quality of the training directly while also receiving another source of revenue from the vouchers.

The Rationale for Discouraging Job Training

As strongly as some program leaders and staff articulate the benefits of short-term job training, others—those at sites that discourage training—feel strongly that it is unhelpful to participants and to program performance.[8] In the words of Peter Cove of America Works:

> You're talking about people who have been failed by the education and training system—they've been failed in high school, they've been failed by other training programs. Ask them how many training programs they've been in. You say to yourself: "They don't need another classroom where they may think they're going to fail. What they need is a success" . . . The job can be a success. That's the first thing—work can build self-esteem and success.

Others noted that, on average, about half of participants drop out of training programs. And even those who complete training programs do not necessarily go directly into jobs.[9] Finally, there is the cost of screening and monitoring that, some said, can be significant. The only motivation for that level of effort, one nonprofit director argued, would be if one would "really be interested [in someone] the way you would about a family member that this person is going to the right school." That effort, he added, was "all without compensation and all under the assumption that somebody's going to . . . get placed in a job that relates to that training which I would say happens less than 10 percent of the time. The majority drop out of the training, or get to the end of the training and come back into a job-search program because no one is helping them get placed."

THE EMPLOYABILITY OF HARD-TO-SERVE INDIVIDUALS

A third area of difference among work-first programs relates to judgments about whether particular hard-to-serve individuals are "employable" or not. As mentioned before, everyone who is assigned to one of the 26 employment programs in New York City has already been evaluated at Job Centers, the city-run welfare offices, to ensure that they are currently employable. Those deemed currently unemployable are referred to specialized programs for drug or alcohol dependency, mental health issues, physical disabilities, illiteracy, language barriers, parents with infant children, or pregnant women.[10]

Once participants arrive at their employment programs, however, staff members sometimes become aware of serious barriers that were not identified at the Job Centers. This can occur when case managers meet with new arrivals during orientation or later in the program as staff members prepare to send people out on job interviews. If serious barriers are detected, staff members have the option to "deassign" individuals from their programs, meaning referring them back to Job Centers for further evaluation and ending their participation in that employment program.

Deassignment rates at most programs range from 5 to 20 percent, with two outliers, both nonprofits, at 39 percent and 42 percent (Figure 7.4). The director of one the outlier programs explained that participants who are not motivated to work are often deassigned from the program. "We just haven't been able to help them," he said. "Maybe someone else [another program] will."

Even excluding these two outliers, the variation in deassignment rates is fairly large. It is unlikely that most of this variation stems from

Figure 7.4 Deassignment Rates among Participants

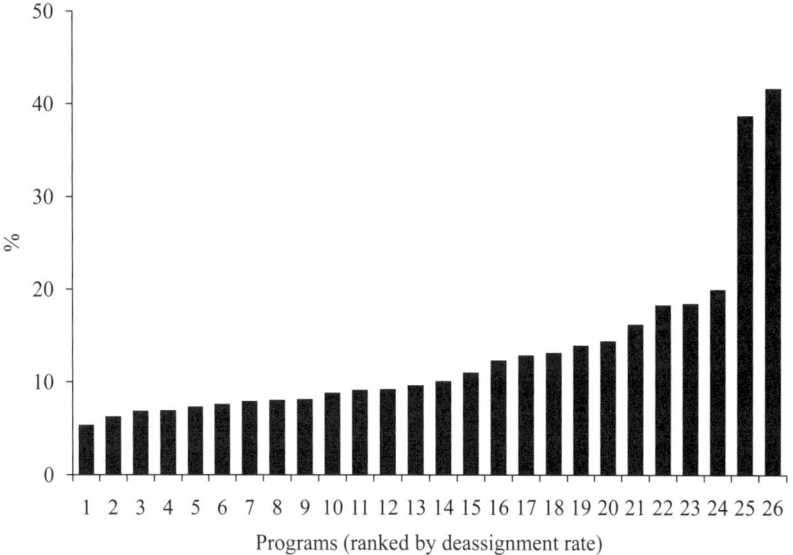

different levels of barriers to employment among participants, given the city's random assignment of participants to programs within their boroughs. (Nor do average deassignment rates vary widely among boroughs.) Instead, it appears that different deassignment rates largely reflect different views among program leaders and staff about the employability of hard-to-serve individuals. Some programs conduct detailed screening for barriers and deassign people with more significant challenges. Others do little screening and assume, in essence, that they can help almost anyone find a job.

Whether people with significant work barriers are better off being deassigned or not is beyond the scope of this study. Some staff members feel that deassignments help participants by connecting them with specialized services elsewhere. An example is a faith-based provider with a fairly high deassignment rate. The orientation facilitator asks new participants to write down their barriers in the form of a letter to her, since she found that it is easier for people to discuss their personal issues in writing.

> You'd be surprised what I get in those letters. Sometimes it's more than I bargained for . . . Then I talk to them one-on-one. If I feel

like it's too much for us to handle as a program, I ask [the case manager] to deassign them and send them where they can actually get the help . . . I don't look it as "I don't want to be bothered—you told me something and now I want to get rid of you." It's not the case. The case is that you need to take care of this.

In contrast, staff at the program with the lowest deassignment rate, a for-profit, purposefully tried to avoid deassignments. The director explained that people with, say, very low basic skills in reading or math could be deassigned from the program, but in her experience, people with low basic skills can often become employed. She also noted that the program tries to resolve certain serious barriers such as homelessness:

We'll say, "How long is it going to take you [to get a housing voucher]?" [They'll say,] "I need the next three weeks." They'll come here everyday until they get that voucher. When they get the voucher we'll give them an excusable absence so they can pick up the voucher, look for housing, and go shopping for their furniture. Once that's done . . . HRA is paying only a portion of their rent so they need a job then.

In terms of screening for barriers, some programs spend more time assessing people when they arrive, so they are more likely to be aware of serious life challenges. At the other end of the spectrum, one for-profit program has no case managers, although a social worker is available. Staff members purposefully do not spend much time on assessment since, in the program's view, case management shifts the focus from what welfare recipients can do to what their limitations are, reducing the momentum towards employment. This for-profit is quick-placement focused, but the data show that programs with a quick-placement focus do not have significantly different deassignment rates than ones with a case-management focus.

Deassignments are an important programmatic feature of New York City's welfare system. Most U.S. cities do not have the range of specialized services for hard-to-serve individuals like New York City does, giving those cities fewer options to deassign individuals from their regular employment programs. Even so, the concept of deassignment does have relevancy across the nation. Every state is allowed to exempt 20 percent of its caseload from federal TANF work requirements. These exemptions can be considered a form of deassignment.

SANCTIONING PARTICIPANTS FOR NONCOMPLIANCE

The final area of difference in the operations of work-first programs relates to their level of strictness, or laxity, when participants break program rules. When participants violate those rules, staff can ask them to leave the program. This is called a "referral to sanctions" (hereafter referred to simply as "sanctioning"), and individuals are sent back to their Job Centers for reevaluation and their welfare benefits may be reduced (although usually are not). The rates of sanctioning among participants who showed up for at least one day to their employment programs and who were not deassigned varies widely, from 36 to 75 percent, with an average of 55 percent (Figure 7.5).

The most frequent reason for sanctioning is that people drop out of their employment programs. Staff estimated that about half of all participants drop out within the first week. Other examples of noncompliance include repeatedly showing up late, not engaging in program activities, and rejecting job offers without cause.

Figure 7.5 Sanctioning Rates among Participants Who Are Not Deassigned

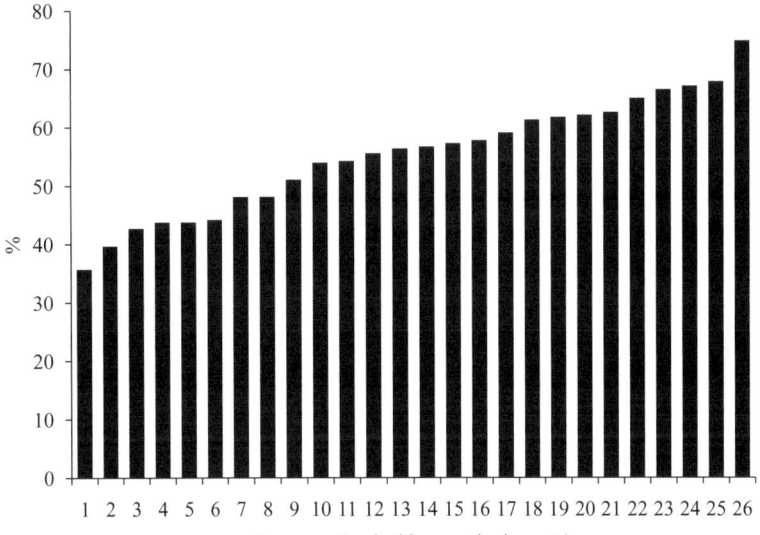

Staff noted that actual rule breaking—whether resulting in sanctioning or not—is very common, since most participants violate rules at some point. For example, consistent attendance is rare and people tend to be truant a few times a month. Sanctions therefore are focused on repeat offenders who are seen as purposefully "gaming the system" to avoid employment or who are being disruptive.

An observer of these employment programs would find it difficult to guess which programs have higher sanction rates than others. Some programs appear stricter about rules than others, but a correlation between perceived strictness and sanctioning is not apparent. Moreover, none of the programs emphasizes the threat of sanctions. According to staff, one reason is that a punitive approach undermines efforts to engage people at the start of a program, especially since many people arrive angry and distrustful. Another reason is that participants, especially longer term welfare recipients, know how to comply "just enough" to avoid breaking the rules. They know, for example, to bring in documentation, such as a doctor's note, to excuse them from extended absences. A final reason is that most participants are aware of New York City's relatively lenient sanction policies, including a conciliation policy that enables most people to avoid actual benefit reductions and, instead, be referred to another employment program.

Since most sanctions stem from dropping out of programs, sanctioning is not fully within the discretion of staff. In other words, participants who drop out "refer themselves to sanctions," as a case manager put it. But staff may be able to influence dropout rates, especially in terms of engagement at the start of the program. In a few cases, the staff's emphases appear to have a noticeable influence on sanction rates. An example is the nonprofit, discussed earlier, that considers the first three days of the program a "probation period" during which the staff assesses participants to determine their legitimate interest in becoming employed. People who are not motivated to work often drop out anyway, the director noted, but those who appear to be unmotivated are sanctioned at their first violation of program rules. He explained:

> It's easier to dismiss someone for concrete, flagrant violations when in fact the real issue (i.e., the source of their lack of motivation) is more complicated than that and can perhaps be turned around in a minority of cases. But there again there's the issue of prudent allocation of staff energies . . . We try to keep (the average

caseload per caseworker) to no more than 50. It usually hovers around 30 because of our high (sanctioning) rate.

This program has the third highest sanction rate. Almost two-thirds of those who show up to this program and are not deassigned end up being sanctioned. At the other end of the spectrum, the director of the program with the third lowest rate (just over 50 percent) tells her employees to keep sanctioning to a minimum. In staff meetings, for example, she asks case managers to explain their rationales for the sanctions they made.[11]

Notes

1. The date of placement used for these calculations is the job start date. The date of hire is not available.
2. Cove added, "Does that mean we don't have a day care problem [in this country]? Of course we have a day care problem." But he argued that employment should be a central component in helping people address their life challenges.
3. The correlation between median days to placement and the number of case managers per capita is −0.03 (P = 0.53).
4. At one program, officewide pressure was created by having teams, each with a job developer, case manager, and retention specialist. Although teams were not given placement targets (to encourage them to share job leads with each other), team performance was posted on the wall to encourage friendly competition. That competition, the director said, is an important driver of performance at the site.
5. Recall that longer term training or on-the-job training are not service options offered in New York City's welfare system, so they are not examined in this volume.
6. On a related point, training can also boost people's confidence, staff said, because, after training, "they have skills and what they have to offer is important to the employer, rather than going out saying 'I just need a job.'"
7. This waiting period was set at two weeks prior to 2005, but high drop-out rates from training programs led the city to extend the waiting period.
8. This is not to say that all staff at these programs agreed. In one case, for example, a job developer felt strongly that his program's focus on direct placement, without any training options, hindered people's opportunities.
9. The exact placement rates are not known because data are not available on which individuals in the study sample received training. What is known, instead, is the total number of individuals, by program, sent to voucher-eligible training.
10. The definition of employability in New York City also includes having child care in place. The city helps people find child care and provides vouchers to pay for it, if needed.

11. If people's noncompliance stem from their barriers to work, such as drug addiction, she emphasized to staff that they should deassign them, not sanction them, so that these individuals could receive specialized help. While this example suggests a negative correlation between sanction rates and deassignment rates, the actual correlation is near zero.

8
Different Practices among Program Types

Another useful way of exploring the main differences between today's work-first employment programs is to look across organizational types. For example, in what ways do nonprofit and for-profit programs differ in their service strategies? Do programs that are compensated solely based on performance—that is, by their success at helping people get and keep jobs—have different practices than programs that are compensated only partly based on performance? And how do program practices differ between large and small programs, or between faith-based and secular ones? The 26 welfare-to-work programs in New York City provide preliminary insights into these issues.

NONPROFIT VERSUS FOR-PROFIT

The views of program leaders illustrate the blurred nature of the categories "nonprofit" and "for-profit." For example, several nonprofits said that they try to run like for-profits. William Forrester, Executive Vice President of Goodwill Industries of Greater New York and Northern New Jersey, explained how his nonprofit organization (which runs three of the 26 sites) draws on for-profit management techniques:

> It's a business. My philosophy is that a nonprofit business is the same as a for-profit business except that our shareholders are the clients we serve everyday . . . We try to model ourselves after a for-profit in the sense that we have a vision, a strategic plan, we do marketing, we hold people to account . . . You have pressures to produce. Then you have the pressures that you want to treat a person with dignity. How long can we spend engaged in counseling and case management? . . . [Spend too much time on that] and your production is down.

Likewise, Karen Smith, Senior Vice President of the nonprofit Wildcat Industries noted, "Nonprofit agencies call themselves nonprofit, but they're really in it for the profit. They just call it something else." Other staff members at nonprofit programs emphasize that covering costs is a challenge but is necessary to stay in business. "You have to have a for-profit mentality because otherwise you won't survive," one staff member said.

But leaders at other nonprofit programs express very different sentiments. Covering costs is not their primary concern, and they are willing to fundraise to address budget shortfalls so they can provide the level of service they believe is appropriate. For example, the director of a small faith-based program recalled the message she received from the nuns who founded the organization:

> Sister Mary Paul and Sister Geraldine were the founders of the program and their model was "You do the work, we'll find the money." I remember Sister Geraldine when we lost a contract and we had no money. [I asked,] "Are we going to close the program?" [She said] "We're not closing the program. We will find the money." And they always did. They had the pressure but they didn't put the pressure on me or on the staff.

Interestingly, the person overseeing a for-profit program, New York Job Partners, discussed how their program philosophy essentially matches that of a nonprofit. New York Job Partners is part of a national company (Affiliated Computer Services) that was new to the social service field and trying to gain a reputation for providing quality services. Charlotte Curan, Operations Manager of their contracts in New York explained, "I've been told to do a super quality program and make it grow. I've gotten the support from [the regional manager]: 'If you need another job developer, hire them' . . . Maybe someone else will make millions of dollars for the company, but right now this line of business has to show the quality services that we can produce."[1]

Staff members at other for-profits, however, emphasize their programs' distinctiveness from their nonprofit counterparts. For example, Pete Cove of America Works said one advantage of for-profits is their greater flexibility in terms of employee compensation, including the use of performance pay. Another advantage, he said, is resource flexibility, meaning being able to adjust program operations quickly in response to changing conditions. And Susan Melocarro of Career and Education Consultants said that pressure to cover costs distinguishes for-profits from nonprofits:

> I'll tell you the difference with the nonprofits. If they are not generating enough revenue from the contract, they do fundraising or they have foundation funds or funds from other sources that subsidize the shortfall. In a private sector business it's not like that . . . So you cannot miss a beat. You have to, as management, be on top of this every day . . . because if you're placement numbers go down, you don't have enough revenue coming in to fund your operation. There's a lot of pressure.

Although one might guess that for-profit providers would downplay their profit motive to participants, that was not the case. Some staff even used their organizations' for-profits status as a selling point during orientations. As one job developer explained:

> [When participants arrive] they're bitter about all the agencies they've been to. I'll say "Look, they are nonprofit organizations. We are a for-profit organization . . . I'm not going to fool you. I'm here for one purpose—to make my company money and make myself money. And if I don't get hires, I don't make bonuses. Do you think I'm going to waste your time and my own sending you to jobs you're not going to get?" . . . They appreciate the honesty.

How do for-profit and nonprofit practices differ? Figure 8.1 shows differences across a range of practices, starting with deassignments. Recall that deassignments occur when staff members believe that certain individuals are currently unemployable. These people are referred back to Job Centers for further evaluation, ending their participation at the employment program. For-profits deassigned participants at almost half the rate of nonprofits.[2] This contradicts conventional wisdom that for-profit service providers are more likely to "cream" the caseload by focusing on the easiest to employ. At least among these programs, for-profits may be more motivated to try to place a broader range of participants into jobs than nonprofits.[3]

Sanctioning, on the other hand, is higher among for-profits, possibly because nonprofits are better at engaging participants, leading to fewer dropouts and more compliance with program rules, but fieldwork shows that the level of engagement appears to be at least as strong

92 Feldman

Figure 8.1 Organizational Practices among Nonprofit and For-Profit Programs

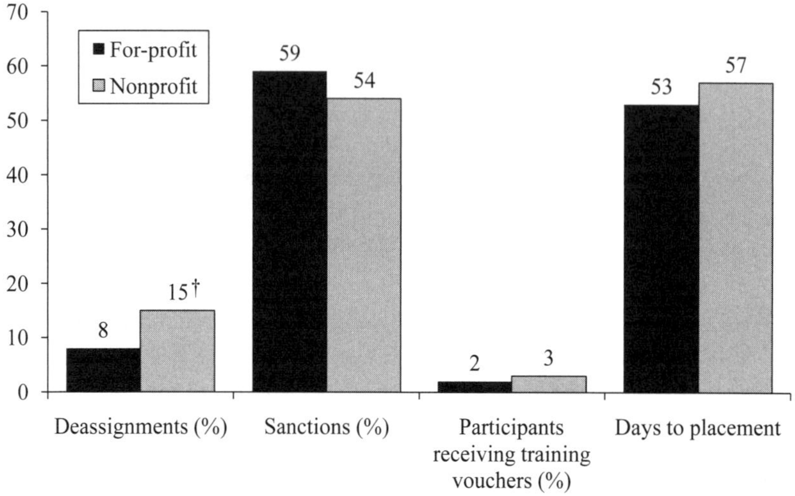

[Bar chart comparing For-profit and Nonprofit programs:
- Deassignments (%): For-profit 8, Nonprofit 15†
- Sanctions (%): For-profit 59, Nonprofit 54
- Participants receiving training vouchers (%): For-profit 2, Nonprofit 3
- Days to placement: For-profit 53, Nonprofit 57]

† Difference is statistically significant at the 0.05 level.

among for-profits. Another possibility is that nonprofits are simply less willing to exert their administrative authority over participants, leading to fewer sanctions.

Few participants are referred to voucher job training at either type of program, although the rate at nonprofits is almost twice as high.[4] Moreover, for-profits have slightly quicker placement speeds, on average—a difference of four days.[5] Interestingly, though, the five fastest sites in terms of placement, as well as the six slowest, are all nonprofits. Nonprofits' wider dispersion in terms of program strategy is discussed in more detail in Chapter 10.

COMPENSATION: FULL VERSUS PARTIAL PERFORMANCE-BASED PAY

Nine small nonprofit community-based organizations (CBOs) in New York City are part of the "EarnFair Alliance" and operate employment programs under the auspices of SEEDCO, a national community development organization. The Alliance began when three of the CBOs decided to begin providing welfare-to-work services. The New York Community Trust, the city's community foundation, gave them a planning grant to develop a partnership in which they, and other CBOs that wanted to join, would apply for a contract with New York City under an umbrella organization. The result was the EarnFair Alliance, with SEEDCO acting as the prime contractor. As a SEEDCO manager explained, the Alliance was designed so that "one central organization managed all of the relationships with the agencies, acted as the primary vendor, and handled the administrative burden of providing these services so that the CBOs could focus on what their strength was, which is providing the case management and the training and also the job development piece."

An important difference between EarnFair programs and other employment service providers in New York City relates to compensation. While New York City pays the nine EarnFair programs solely based on performance, just as it does for the other employment programs, the Alliance has a unique compensation arrangement. SEEDCO pools EarnFair programs' revenues (i.e., their placement and retention milestone payments) and redistributes those funds back to these nine programs using a formula that is only partially performance based. In particular, half of the compensation is based on line-item compensation for expenses and the other half is based on performance in terms of milestone achievements.[6] The rationale for this payment structure relates to the fact that performance-based contracts necessitate waiting for compensation until contractual milestones are achieved. The Alliance's payment structure allows small, capital-constrained CBOs to enter into performance-based contracts with the city while still funding current operations. From a research perspective, this arrangement allows us to compare the practices of programs (those in the Alliance) that receive partial performance pay with others (those not in the Alliance) whose compensation is solely based on performance.

EarnFair members have autonomy to run their own programs, but SEEDCO sets employment and retention goals, provides technical assistance, and conducts semi-annual audits to ensure that EarnFair programs' case files meet the standards set by New York City. "It keeps you on your toes," a program director said. "They don't want to wait until we have a VendorStat meeting with HRA to identify the problems we are having with the files or the numbers [performance levels]." Moreover, SEEDCO organizes monthly program design meetings in which staff from the nine programs exchange ideas about useful practices. And EarnFair members have access to SEEDCO's job development capacity. SEEDCO operates EarnFair LLC, a social purpose business that runs a temporary-help agency to connect disadvantaged workers with companies needing entry-level workers. One director estimated that 20 percent of her program's placements came from these leads.

EarnFair programs that do not meet their milestone goals are put into "corrective action" and receive more intensive assistance. The director of one site that was in the middle of a corrective action explained that SEEDCO had provided a full-time staff person during the turnaround period to help the program examine their internal processes and restructure their job responsibilities.

Figure 8.2 compares the organizational practices of EarnFair sites with those of other programs. Deassignment rates are higher among EarnFair programs, while referrals to sanctions are lower.[7] EarnFair programs rarely refer participants to job training—1 percent received training vouchers, on average. One reason may be that these small

Figure 8.2 Organizational Practices among EarnFair Programs and Other Programs

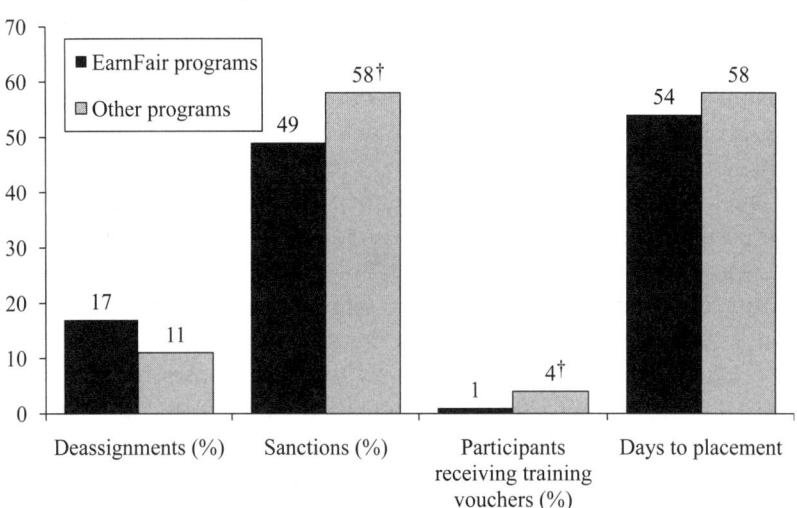

† Difference is statistically significant at the 0.05 level.

CBOs cannot afford to have specialized staff to focus on helping participants choose and apply for training courses, as some of the larger programs can do.

The figure also shows that EarnFair programs have somewhat faster placement speeds than other programs, but the pattern of placement speeds across programs shows little consistency. In fact, one EarnFair program has the fastest speeds among the 26 programs in the city, while another has the second slowest. Fieldwork also shows that some EarnFair programs emphasized quick-placement while others emphasized job-readiness assistance. This variance in strategy underscores the autonomy these providers have to design and operate their own programs.

PROGRAM SIZE

Size is the most obvious difference one notices when spending time in the city's employment programs. Some programs take up whole floors of large office buildings, with dozens of staff members and classrooms filled with participants. At other programs, an entire new cohort of participants can sit around a single table during orientation, and the program comprises only a few rooms. Figure 8.3 shows the variation in the average size of new cohorts in the 26 programs.[8] Most programs range from about 20 to 90 new entrants every two weeks, although one program has an average cohort of 175.

Interestingly, staff members at both large and small sites see benefits to their programs' size.[9] For example, those at larger programs said they are better able to cater to companies that have large job orders—say, a hospital that needs 20 custodians. These staff members see large job orders as important for getting people employed quickly. A job developer at a larger program noted:

> We're pumping fast—a volume place. You [an employer] might as well take 10 people in one week from me. Great! I just cleared out 10 more people. There's nothing wrong with high volume. And they're not garbage jobs. They are things they [participants] ask for specifically. I have a ton of people working in home health aide right now . . . You start off on the first tier, then you go to CNA

[Certified Nursing Assistant], then you can go to LPN [Licensed Practical Nurse], then you can go to RN [Registered Nurse]. Next thing you know you could make $40, $50 an hour.

Program leaders also said that size was an advantage in terms being able to weather funding fluctuations.

Staff members at smaller programs, on the other hand, see at least two advantages of their size. One is communication. With smaller caseloads, details about participants' needs and progress can be shared quickly among the staff. One staff member had recently moved from a larger program to a smaller one. She explained how information from the job developer would "eventually get back to the case manager, but there was a lag time there . . . Here we instantly know. We're constantly discussing with [the program director]: 'What do you think about this person?' We're discussing it within [the staff]." In her view, organizational size, not just different management emphases, led to better communication and teamwork.

Another advantage of smaller programs is that engaging participants and building trust is easier because participants receive more individual attention. "Our groups are a lot smaller [than most programs]

Figure 8.3 Number of Participants per Program (average size of group arriving every two weeks)

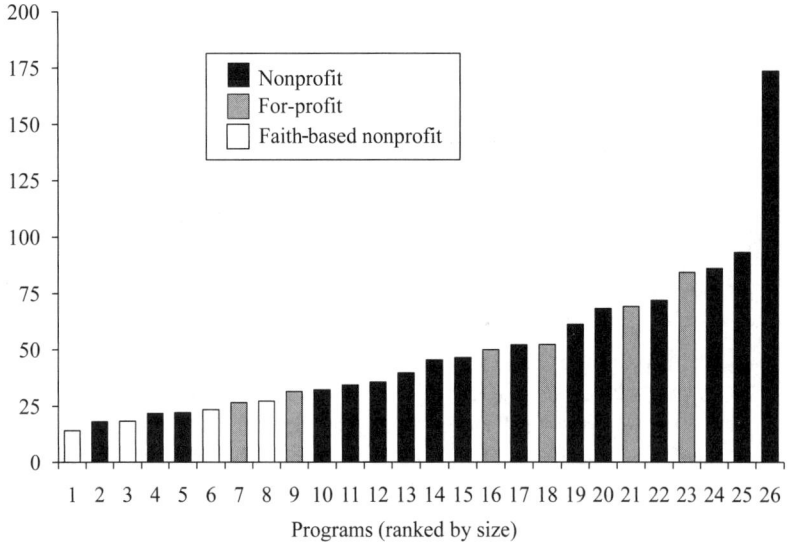

and it gives us the opportunity to get more personal with them," a case manager explained. "There's a lot of motivation [among participants] that first day." Moreover, staff at larger programs may be more specialized, making people "feel like you're passing them around a little," as a staff member at a smaller program put it. "The case manager does this, the job developer does that. See this person, see that person."

To examine program practices by size, sites can be grouped into categories of small, medium, and large, each with 8 to 10 programs in it.[10] As Figure 8.4 shows, deassignment rates are higher, on average, among smaller programs. This could occur if smaller programs provide more in-depth screening for barriers to work. Sanctioning, on the other hand, is lower among smaller programs, possibly because these programs are better able to engage participants, or because smaller, community-based programs are less willing to exert authority over participants by enforcing rules of behavior.

The third variable, use of training, rises with program size. This may relate to staffing capacity. Midsize and larger programs that encourage

Figure 8.4 Organizational Practices among Programs of Different Sizes

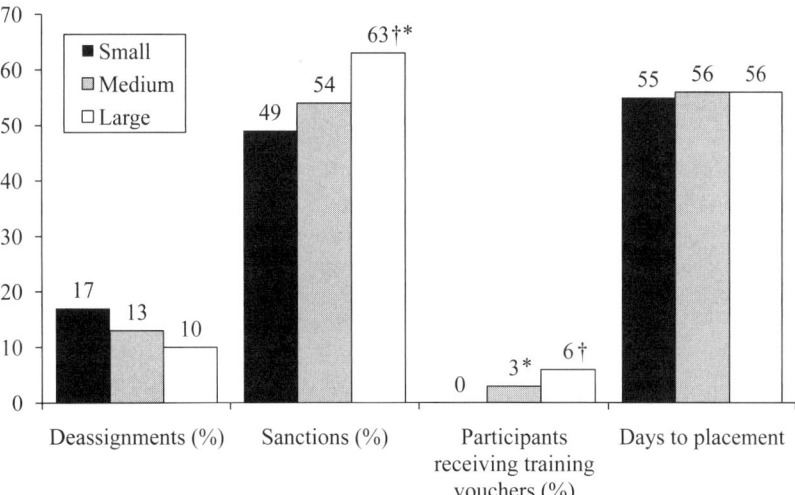

† Difference between large and small programs is statistically significant at the 0.05 level.
* Difference between that size category and one smaller is statistically significant at the 0.10 level.

training often have "training specialists" that help connect people to training programs. When asked how more staff might help, for example, a job developer at a small faith-based program said it would boost placements, produce better job matches, and help "get them into a training program." "It's hard, believe me," she said, in describing the work of running a program with three staff members and a director. "I'm tired right now."

Finally, the results for placement speeds imply that a program's decision to emphasize quick-placement versus barrier-removal is not dependent on its size. All three groups have similar average placement speeds.

FAITH-BASED VERSUS SECULAR

Four of the 26 programs are run by faith-based (Christian) organizations. Faith-based providers working under pay-for-performance social service contracts are not well studied, so even this limited sample provides some helpful preliminary insights. Surprisingly, staff at faith-based programs did not emphasize, or even usually mention, religious factors in describing their work. This may reflect, in part, sensitivity to controversies surrounding the use of faith-based providers as government contractors. Most staff at faith-based sites said they viewed their organizations as "regular" nonprofits that happened to be part of religiously affiliated organizations. For example, a case manager at one faith-based program was asked if there were any ways to tell that the program was run by a Christian organization. She answered:

> I don't think so. I'm actually Jewish, but the organization is Catholic. I've worked for a couple other nonprofits and it seems pretty similar to me, except that we have next Friday off for Good Friday. I appreciate the history of the organization and where it comes from, but I don't feel like it has any direct effect on what we do.

The director of this program expressed a similar sentiment, saying that, although the parent organization was founded by nuns, its current leadership was lay and it is essentially "just a nonprofit." Staff at the other faith-based sites echoed these comments. "It's no different," said one case manager. "If you see a difference, it's a problem from my perspective."

An executive at one faith-based site, however, explained that his program's commitment to serving the community was difficult to jibe with the demands of implementing a performance-based contract. "We are a community development corporation and it just happens to be that we're faith-based," he said. "Maybe as a faith-based organization we bring to the table certain sensitivities that other organizations may not, but those sensitivities in many instances have gotten us in trouble because you do have to operate as a business." He noted that the program's parent organization was subsidizing the contract with New York City because the program was not able to cover costs:

> If we were really a nuts and bolts for-profit or not-for-profit organization where the fiscal piece is the bottom line, we would drop [the contract]. But we've made that commitment . . . Therein lies, I think, the major difference between a regular organization and a faith-based one. You have to go beyond the bottom line, which is a fiscal one.

On the other hand, a different faith-based program has a much different philosophy, with a focus on meeting financial targets and getting people into jobs quickly. In fact, it has the fastest placement rates among all 26 programs in the city. It is also the only one with an explicit strategy (or at least the only one whose staff was willing to discuss it) to try to reemploy participants just before their retention milestone dates. The staff calls participants the week before their milestone dates to check if they are still employed. If not, they encourage them to come to the program office that week to be placed into a new job. This approach is within the rules of the contract with New York City, although some might see it as gaming the contract. In any case, this program's focus on achieving milestone payments, in contrast with the prior program discussed, shows the diversity in program philosophy among faith-based providers.

Interestingly, religion was mentioned several times, unprompted, by staff at programs that are not faith based. Some individuals explained how faith is a central part of their lives, both as a source of emotional support in a challenging line of work and a source of inspiration that participants' troubles can be overcome. In a few cases, staff said they spoke about faith with participants. "We pray," said a job developer at a small secular nonprofit. "People give their life to Christ. People start going to church. I have people who have stopped drinking." She emphasized that turning around people's lives was much more than just giving people a job. At another secular program, a workshop facilitator described show she tries to inspire people by drawing on a higher power:

> I use inspiration. We talk about the Lord. I don't go into religion but I always speak about what has worked for me. There's a higher power and we have to tap into that higher power each and every day of our lives . . . I don't use the term religion. I use the term inspiration. Let's inspire each other. I tell them, "Let's ask for that. Let's ask for a higher power to intervene in this new start and let's all come together as one."

Comparing the practices of faith-based and secular providers, Figure 8.5 shows that, like other nonprofits, these faith-based programs deassign at a higher rate but sanction at a lower rate.[11] Also, like other smaller nonprofits, training is not encouraged at faith-based programs. The two groups are quite similar, however, in terms of their average

Figure 8.5 Organizational Practices among Faith-Based and Non-Faith-Based Programs

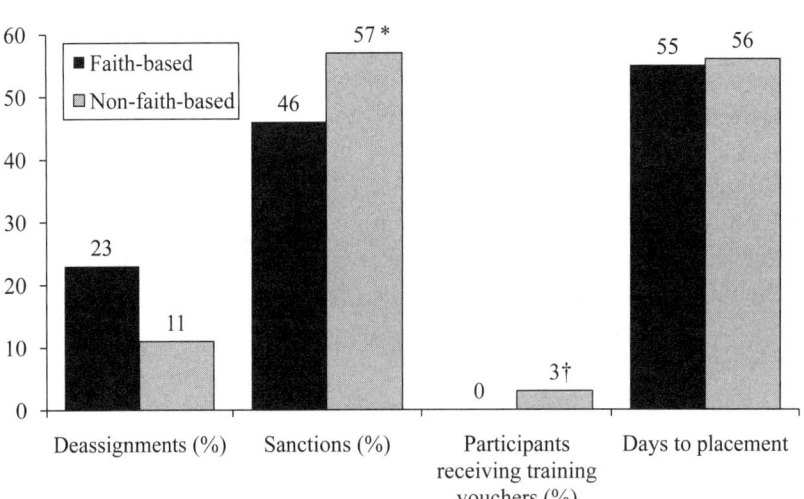

† Difference is statistically significant at the 0.05 level.
* Difference is statistically significant at the 0.10 level.

placement speeds, with a median days-to-placement (55 days) that is only two days faster than other programs. But that average reflects wide diversity in placement speeds among faith-based providers (as with secular ones too), including the site with the fastest placement speed and the site that is the second slowest.

Notes

1. This example recalls the observation by Eggleston, Miller, and Zeckhauser (2001) that "when reputation is an asset, for-profits may act like altruistic nonprofits, using quality as an instrument of competition."
2. Without the two outlier sites (both nonprofits) with high deassignment rates, the average deassignment rate for nonprofits drops from 15 to 12 percent versus 8 percent at for-profit programs.
3. The use of random assignment reduces the chances that these differences are a result of participant characteristics. Moreover, for-profits have a lower deassignment rate even after controlling for observable participant characteristics.
4. The denominator for these training-usage rates excludes anyone who was deassigned or sanctioned. (Recall that most people who are sanctioned either never showed up or dropped out within a few days.)
5. Specifically, the average among for-profit programs in terms of median number of days to placement (the number of days it takes to place half of a program's participants into jobs, among participants who get jobs) is 53 days. The average among nonprofit programs is 57 days.
6. Each year SEEDCO asks the nine organizations to estimate how many participants they will serve that year and to create a line-item budget for providing placement and retention services. Once the budget is approved, SEEDCO pays 50 percent of those costs via monthly payments. (Alliance members have to submit monthly expense reports to SEEDCO.) The other 50 percent of Alliance members' revenues is performance based and tied to their milestone achievements. SEEDCO provides lower milestone payments compared to the HRA payment because these milestones are only meant to cover 50 percent of costs (the other half being covered by line-item reimbursement). The end result is that members receive about the same amount of money as they would if they contracted directly with HRA, but they get half the money in advance.
7. The difference in deassignment rates is not driven by the two outlier sites with high deassignment rates. One of the outliers is an EarnFair member but the other is not. Excluding both from the sample, EarnFair members deassign 14 percent while other programs deassign 9 percent. The higher deassignment rates at EarnFair sites may result from more thorough screening of participants because these programs are partially compensated for doing intake and assessment. It could also be that these programs feel less need to place hard-to-serve participants because their pay is less tied to milestone achievement, or that they feel more flexibility to

deassign people whom they believe would be better served by other, more specialized programs.
8. These data show the flow into programs. Data on the stock, or the average number of participants in programs, are not available.
9. Some interviewees had worked at other programs, so they could compare across programs of different sizes.
10. Categories are created by dividing programs using natural breakpoints in the data. Results of the "large" category are very similar if the especially large (outlier) program is excluded.
11. Without the outlier programs in terms of deassignments (one of which is faith based), the two groups are closer, but still seven percentage points apart.

Part 3

Explaining Performance Differences among Work-First Employment Programs

9
What Works within Work-First?

The last two chapters described the main differences in strategy and structure among the 26 work-first employment programs in New York City. Now we turn to the subject of effectiveness. Which of those organizational differences helps explain performance differences among programs? In other words, why are some of today's work-first programs more successful at helping people become and stay employed?

Outcome data show that performance varies considerably among the programs. For example, the job placement rate varies from 9 to 29 percent. Another performance measure is employment retention. The share of placed participants that is still working six months after joining the program (at any job, not necessarily the original one) ranges from 42 to 74 percent.

The best measure of overall performance is termed the "caseload employment rate" in this study. It is the share of all participants (not just placed ones) that becomes employed and is still working at any job six months later. This measure ranges from 4 to 12 percent—three times higher at the top-performing program than the bottom. The fact that individuals are randomly assigned to programs within their boroughs makes it likely that organizational practices, rather than demographic factors, are the main driver of these performance differences.

At the same time, these statistics illustrate the stark challenge—in New York City and across the nation—of helping welfare recipients achieve sustained work. Even at the most successful program in the city, only 12 out of every 100 participants are able to become and stay employed for at least six months. Innovations in the design and management of employment and training policies for low-income Americans are clearly needed to ratchet up performance. Evidence about which practices are more effective than others among today's employment programs can help further that goal.

The findings in this chapter are based on data from the more than 14,000 participants assigned to programs during the sample period who showed up for at least a day to their programs. In many cases, separate results are discussed for custodial and noncustodial individuals. Results for custodial individuals are the most relevant to national policy because the vast majority of welfare recipients in the United States are custodial parents. But results for noncustodial individuals are relevant to important policy efforts in the nation as well, including those designed to reduce prison recidivism by providing employment services to ex-convicts, most of whom are noncustodial men.

To investigate effective practices among programs, this study uses regression analysis. This statistical technique models the relationship between a dependent variable (such as participants' employment outcomes) and independent variables (including program characteristics). In particular, multilevel logistic regressions are used. Logistic regressions are useful when dependent variables are constrained between two outcomes, such as whether participants are placed in jobs or not. Moreover, multilevel models take into account the nested structure of the data, with participants grouped by employment programs. Further methodological details are provided in Appendix A, and Appendix C provides a sample of the regression results. The rest of this chapter presents the key findings based on the regression results as well as those based on more simple cross tabulations.

FACTORS THAT AFFECT PERFORMANCE

For-Profit versus Nonprofit

Comparing outcomes of for-profit and nonprofit employment programs in New York City shows that the six for-profit programs have better overall results. Figure 9.1 shows that participants have a higher probability of obtaining jobs when they are assigned to for-profit sites than to nonprofit ones.[1] In particular, the placement rate among for-profits (24 percent) is seven percentage points higher, on average, than among nonprofits (17 percent), a difference of more than a third. Among people who become employed, however, nonprofits have a larger share that enters high wage jobs, as defined by the HRA. They also have better six-month employment retention rates among placed individuals.[2] But using the best measure of overall performance—the share of all

Figure 9.1 Performance of For-Profit and Nonprofit Programs

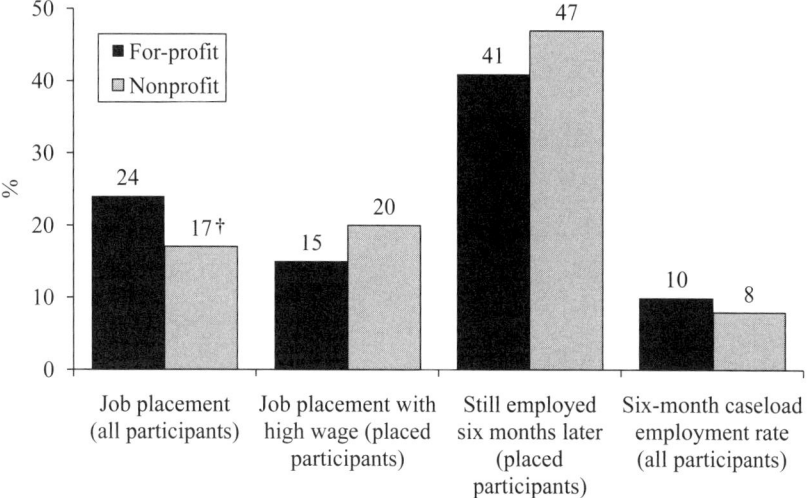

† Difference is statistically significant at the 5% level.

participants who become employed and are still working six months later—for-profits have a two-percentage-point advantage over nonprofits (10 percent versus 8 percent), a difference of 25 percent, although it is not statistically significant (P = 0.12). The figure shows the results for the full sample, but the relative performance of nonprofits and for-profits is similar for custodial and noncustodial subgroups.

Figure 9.2 shows the average number of milestones achieved per 100 participants, based on programs' contract with the city, including the potential to earn one placement milestone and two retention milestones per participant. For-profits achieve more than a third more milestones than nonprofits (48 versus 35).[3] By getting more people into jobs, for-profits earn more placement milestones and—despite their lower employment-retention rates—earn more retention milestones as well.

If we controlled for organizational practices such as the use of training and an emphasis on case management versus quick placement, would we still see performance differences between nonprofits and for-profits? This question may be more of interest to management scholars than practitioners, but it is another way of examining what makes nonprofit and for-profit programs different. To investigate the question,

Figure 9.2 Average Number of Placement and Retention Milestones Achieved per 100 Participants

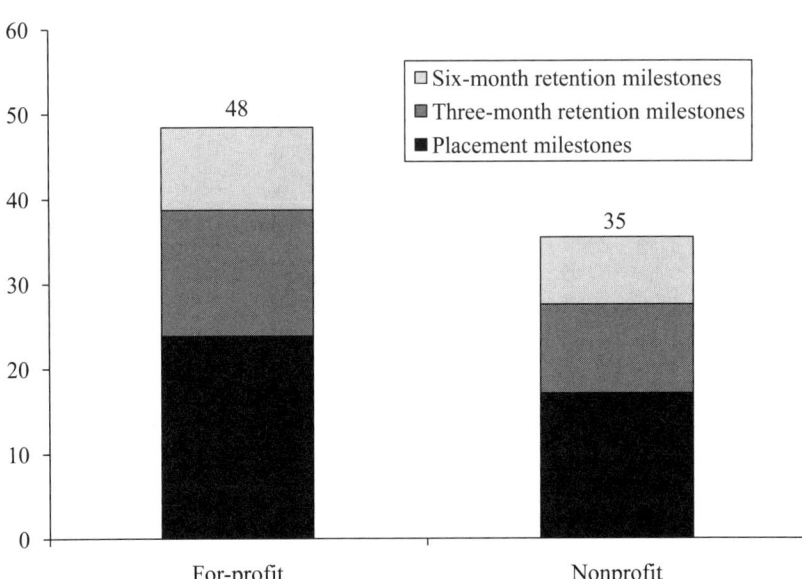

regression analysis can be used to isolate the effect of organizational form, while also controlling for demographic differences among programs' participants. The results show no statistically significant differences between nonprofits and for-profits in the chances that an individual (custodial or noncustodial) will be placed in a job, nor that they will find a job and still be working six months later. Because of large standard errors, however, we cannot say if there is an actual difference in performance between these two types of providers. So, although the raw data show performance differences between for-profit and nonprofit programs, once we control for organizational practices, there are no clear inherent differences between these two categories of providers.

Stronger versus Weaker Performance Incentives

To examine the effect of performance incentives, we can compare the outcomes of participants served by the nine programs in the EarnFair Alliance with those served by other programs. Recall that EarnFair programs receive compensation based partly on their results (that is, on their participants' employment and retention outcomes) and partly on their expenses. All other programs are paid solely based on results. Regression analysis is used to isolate the effect of this difference in pay structure from other differentiating factors measured in this study, such as demographics, use of training, and a focus on quick placement versus case management.

The results imply that stronger incentives for performance produce better overall employment results. Put another way, EarnFair programs have less success in helping individuals find and keep jobs. For custodial individuals, for example, being served by an EarnFair site lowers the chances of placement by almost five percentage points, a 22 percent reduction.[4] Noncustodial individuals are also less likely to become employed when served by EarnFair sites, and in fact, the negative effect carries over into employment retention as well for them. Although speculative, having less performance-based pay may lead programs to be less aggressive in terms of retention services.[5] If so, though, it is unclear why this would have a greater effect on noncustodial individuals than custodial ones.

Finally, the results for the full sample show that being served by an EarnFair site reduces one's chances of becoming employed and still working six months later by about three percentage points, or 38 percent. For custodial participants, the effect is negative, but the estimate is not precise enough to say whether it is meaningful. For noncustodial participants, the effect is negative and statistically significant.

Might other characteristics of EarnFair sites contribute to these outcomes? EarnFair programs are smaller than average, being local CBOs, so they may face greater challenges in terms of access to capital and economies of scale. Staffing data show, however, that if capitalization is an issue, it does not affect staffing capacity, which is similar to other programs on a per-participant basis. Moreover, organizational size has no statistically significant correlation with any of the performance measures. So, although we cannot definitively say that the EarnFair sites' form of compensation is the main cause of their lower performance, it is a plausible candidate.

Immediate Job Search versus Short-Term Job Training

The results point to the benefits of immediate job search over short-term, classroom-based training prior to job search, undermining the idea that this type of training facilitates job entry by boosting people's skills or by providing a signal to employers of people's abilities.[6] In terms of placement rates, for example, the results imply that increasing the share of custodial participants that receives training by one percentage point reduces the chance of placement by 0.8 percentage points, a 4 percent reduction. The effect for noncustodial participants is also negative, although somewhat smaller. The apparent negative effect of training on placement, at least for custodial individuals, could stem from several factors. For example, the training itself could be of low value, or programs that encourage training could use other practices that lead to fewer placements, such as conveying less urgency about employment.[7] Fieldwork did not highlight a particular answer.

Turning to employment retention, a greater use of training by programs reduces the chances of six-month employment retention for both custodial and noncustodial individuals who are placed into jobs, although the effect is stronger and statistically significant only for the latter group. For them, each percentage point increase in the share of the caseload that is referred to training reduces retention rates by 1.3 percentage points, or about 3 percent. The finding that a greater use of training reduces programs' employment retention results is surprising. It contradicts the argument that short-term training is an effective way to promote more sustained employment, either by allowing people to obtain more desirable jobs or more confidence on the job. Again, fieldwork did not point to a particular answer.[8]

A caveat to these retention-related findings is that two sites, both run by the same organization, have relatively high rates of training usage and unusually steep drop-offs in retention between three and six months after placement.[9] One of the sites appeared to be poorly run, with visible disorganization. When these two sites are excluded, the effect of training at six months for noncustodial participants is smaller and statistically insignificant. For custodial participants, the effect becomes slightly positive but remains statistically insignificant. In short, even if we disregard the two programs that are especially ineffective at retention, there is still no clear positive effect of training on employment retention.

Finally, in terms of programs' abilities to get people into jobs and keep them working for at least six months, the effect of training is negative and statistically significant for both custodial and noncustodial participants. In fact, for custodial individuals, the use of training is the only program characteristic that has a statistically significant effect on this key outcome measure.[10] Increasing referrals to training by a percentage point is estimated to reduce participants' chances of achieving sustained employment by 0.5 percentage points or about 6 percent.[11]

A Quick-Placement Approach versus a Case-Management Approach

All of the programs provide some case management and coaching, including job interview preparation. But following these initial activities, the results for the full sample show that a quick-placement focus is more beneficial to individuals than an emphasis on case management. In particular, the latter emphasis reduces the chances of job placement as well as the chances that people find jobs and are still working six months later.

That being said, in some cases, a healthy amount of case management can be useful, at least for custodial individuals. For them, the results imply that more case management initially has a positive effect on people's chances of job placement (including placement at a high wage) but with a diminishing return.[12] This reflects the fact that some of the most successful programs are not among the fastest in terms of placement speeds, but they are in the medium to medium-fast range. For sites that provide an average level of case management, though, further increases in case management reduce placement rates. The results imply, for example, that programs that move from providing an average amount of case management (fiftieth percentile in terms of placement speed) to an above-average amount (seventy-fifth percentile) reduce the probability of participants' placement by one percentage point, or just over 4 percent.[13] For noncustodial individuals, the effect of case management on job placement rates is more strongly negative.

The results also show that the amount of case management provided has little effect on employment retention among placed individuals, at least by the six-month mark. Recall that some staff felt that more intensive case management prior to job search helps people stabilize their lives and deal with barriers to work, thus facilitating job retention once employed. The evidence does not support this view.

On the most important measure of performance, the ability of programs to get people working and have them still working at least six months later, more case management has a negative effect for noncustodial individuals. For them, attending a program that provides above-average amount of case management reduces their chances of achieving six months of employment by 0.7 percentage points or 8 percent.[14] For custodial individuals, the effect is negative but smaller and not statistically significant. Overall, then, we can say that a case-management approach either has a negative effect on sustained employment or has no clear positive effect, depending on the type of participant.

FACTORS THAT DO NOT DRIVE PERFORMANCE

Some organizational characteristics turn out to have little or no apparent effect on performance, even though they are areas of obvious difference among programs.

Deassignment Rates

Programs that deem participants to be currently unemployable can deassign them and refer them back to the city-run Job Centers for further evaluation. As we saw earlier, deassignment rates vary considerably among programs. Do higher deassignment rates boost programs' results by enabling staff to focus their energy on those with a better chance of becoming employed? Or do fewer deassignments boost results because some people with more serious barriers can still become employed? The results suggest that the answer to these questions is "neither." Deassignment rates do not noticeably impact longer term performance. Although higher deassignment rates lead to lower placement rates, they also boost employment retention among those who get jobs. Overall, a program's deassignment rate has a statistically insignificant effect on participants' chances of finding a job and staying employed for at least six months.

Program Size

Field research suggests no consistent patterns in terms of organizational practices by program size. For example, programs that emphasize quick placement are run by both small CBOs and large social service agencies. The same goes for programs that emphasize case management. Maybe not surprisingly, then, there are no significant relationships between program size and performance. Some researchers have expressed concerns that CBOs may have difficulty competing for welfare-to-work contracts, given the scale of the task of moving welfare recipients into employment. For example, Grønbjerg (2001) argues "large, multiservice agencies will do better because they have flexibility and discretion in how to allocate their many funding sources among program activities." Small CBOs, on the other hand, "tend to be undercapitalized, cannot easily alter their service mix, and are politically weak, but they often provide niche services targeted at a specific neighborhood or client group." But the evidence from New York City suggests that large employment programs do not have a consistent performance advantage over smaller ones. Some of the lowest performing programs, in fact, are run by large multiservice agencies, as are some of the top-performing ones. Small CBOs have a wide range of performance results as well, including one that has the fourth-highest rate of total milestones achieved per participant (a proxy for both performance and revenues) as well as two at the very bottom. Smaller programs, in other words, can compete with larger programs if they use effective practices.

Sanctioning Rates

When programs sanction individuals for breaking program rules, their participation is terminated and they are referred back to their Job Centers. The rate at which programs impose sanctions varies considerably among programs, as we saw earlier, yet these rates are not significantly correlated with placement or retention rates. One possible reason is that individuals who are sanctioned might have been unlikely to have become employed anyway. As a result, employment programs with lower sanction rates may not necessarily have higher placement rates. Past research has also found little or no effect of an emphasis on adjudication for noncooperative participants or actual rates of sanctioning on the performance of welfare-to-work programs (Mead 1983, 1997; Mitchell, Chadwin, and Nightingale 1980; Riccio and Orenstein 1996).

Does it not matter, then, whether programs are stricter or more lenient in terms of enforcing program rules and workplace norms? Not necessarily. Some programs may set high expectations about behavior while choosing not to use the threat of sanctions to enforce them. This may be particularly true in New York, where the state's sanction rules are relatively lenient. Because the likelihood of benefit cuts as a result of noncompliance is lower than in most states, staff may choose other ways of enforcing rules.

Faith-Based versus Secular Programs

Faith-based programs show little commonality in their approaches. For example, one program has the fastest placement speed among all the sites and is clearly "number focused" in terms of achieving performance goals. Another has the second-slowest placement speed and has a strong commitment to case management. In other words, being faith-based tells us little about organizational practices. Correlations between faith-based status and outcomes imply a lower placement rate among these providers, but there are no clear connections with longer term results.

RESULTS BY GENDER

Nationally less than 10 percent of welfare recipients are male because most welfare systems require adult recipients to be custodial parents. As a result, little research exists on the effects of welfare-to-work programs for men. Although now quite dated, some evidence comes from one of the first rigorously evaluated welfare-to-work programs, the Supported Work Demonstration, which ran in the 1970s. The program produced large positive effects on women's earnings, while men had only small gains (Hollister, Kemper, and Maynard, 1984). Men in the sample were all ex-addicts or ex-offenders.

New York City's welfare system is a useful setting to investigate the role of gender in welfare-to-work programs because, unlike most welfare systems, it has an assistance program for the noncustodial poor called the Safety Net Program. In New York City, these individuals are mandated to participate in employment programs, just like other welfare recipients. As a result, 31 percent of participants in the 26 employment programs are men.[15]

The data show that men and women in the programs have similar employment outcomes, on average. Men have slightly higher placement rates, but lower employment retention. As a result, the share of participants who find jobs and are still working at least six months later is essentially identical (8 percent) for both men and women. Moreover, an examination of how program practices affect men and women shows no evidence of important differences by gender in terms of how those practices affect outcomes. The results contradict what may be conventional wisdom that poor men fare poorly, relative to women, in employment programs.

THE EFFECTS OF ADOPTING BETTER PRACTICES

The results in this chapter imply that programs that adopt more effective practices within work first can see a substantial boost in their outcomes, including on the most important measure of performance in this study: getting participants into jobs and having them still be employed at least six months later. For example, cutting training usage from the seventy-fifth percentile among programs (8 percent of participants referred to training) to the twenty-fifth percentile (no one referred to training) boosts custodial participants' chances of sustained employment by four percentage points, or by more than 45 percent. The effect for noncustodial participants is similar. Switching to a quicker placement approach, meanwhile—increasing placement speed from the seventy-fifth percentile (67 days to place the median placed individual in a job) to the twenty-fifth percentile (47 days)—raises performance by almost 18 percent for noncustodial participants and by slightly less for the full sample.

The findings also have implications for public agencies that contract with service providers. Moving from a compensation scheme based partly on performance to one that is fully performance-based increases sustained employment by more than half (55 percent) for noncustodial participants and by more than a third (35 percent) for the full sample.

What is the predicted effect of changing these three practices at once? The results for the full sample suggest that the combined effect of using less training, becoming more focused on quick placement, and moving from partial to full performance-based pay would more than double the share of participants that get and keep jobs for at least six months, from 6 percent to almost 14 percent. This increase in performance, in a large welfare system such as New York City's, would result in thousands more individuals achieving sustained employment each year. Even so, the fact that even with these "best practices," only 14 percent of participants in the city's programs would achieve employment and still be working six months later is sobering. It is a reminder of the urgent challenge in antipoverty policy, both in New York City and elsewhere, of finding better ways to help welfare recipients become employed and, especially, to stay employed. Moreover, for New York in particular, the fact that almost a third of individuals assigned to employment programs in the city do not show up, and about half of those that do attend drop out within a week, makes connecting those individuals with work more difficult. Strengthening sanctioning policy in New York, even to national averages, could reduce noncompliance with welfare rules and promote greater engagement with welfare-to-work programs, factors that could boost employment rates.

Notes

1. Note that the six-month employment rates (10 percent and 8 percent) in Figure 9.1 are higher than the overall average shown earlier in Figure 2.2 (6 percent) because Figure 9.1 uses participants (those who showed up for at least a day to their programs) as the denominator, whereas Figure 2.2 uses all individuals referred to programs.
2. At the three-month mark, for-profits have a slight advantage, with an employment retention rate of 64 percent versus 63 percent for nonprofits.
3. In dollar terms, for-profit programs earn about 25 percent more revenue per participant, on average, than nonprofit programs under their contract with the city, due to for-profits' greater milestone achievement.
4. Regression results in this chapter apply to the modal participant in the sample.
5. Alternatively, they might be less aggressive at verifying employment retention, meaning obtaining documentation from participants to prove that they are still working. That documentation is required in order for programs to receive payments from the city for reaching those retention milestones.

6. Available data include the percentage of participants at each program that are referred to training, but not which specific individuals received training or if they completed their training programs. Anecdotally, staff said that many participants drop out of training—around half, in some cases.
7. Another possibility is that individuals who complete training programs may be more selective in their job searches, focused on particular jobs in the fields of their training, and this could delay or hinder placements. Although that is possible, it was not discussed as a concern by any of the staff interviewed.
8. Employment programs often try to steer participants to training programs that have job development staff, so that when individuals finish the training, the training program staff (rather than the employment program staff) will help them find a job. One possibility is that training programs make poorer job matches, leading to worse employment retention.
9. Interestingly, the executive overseeing both programs set staff goals for three-month retention rates but not six-month rates.
10. If we exclude the two sites that encourage training and have particularly weak employment retention results, the marginal effect for custodial participants becomes smaller and is no longer statistically significant. For noncustodial individuals, the marginal effect remains the same and is still statistically significant. In short, the results show that this type of short-term training, at least as implemented in New York City, does not produce more sustained employment and may substantially reduce it.
11. It is worth noting that these findings, as with all of those in this chapter, relate to near-term employment outcomes. Longer term follow-up data might show different results for short-term, classroom-based training. Even so, the type of training used, typically lasting a few weeks to three months, allows staff several months to try to place participants into jobs once they complete training. Recall that programs are given six months to place participants in jobs before they are re-randomly assigned to other programs.
12. Without the squared term, the marginal effect is negative (-0.001) and is less statistically significant, with a z-value of 0.08 compared to 0.02 with the squared term.
13. Specifically, the model predicts this effect when moving from a median days-to-placement at the fiftieth percentile for custodial individuals (57 days) to the seventy-fifth percentile (65 days). The combined marginal effect of moving from the twenty-fifth percentile of placement speeds (46 days) to the median (57 days) only increases the chances of placement slightly, from 24.1 to 24.3 percent. Going from a low level of case management to a modest level, in other words, has little effect on performance.
14. Specifically, this means attending a program whose median placement speed is a week longer than average, as compared to one at the average.
15. Much of the analysis in this chapter presents separate results for custodial and noncustodial aid recipients. Custodial participants are mostly female (89 percent) whereas the majority of noncustodial participants are male (58 percent). Here, though, we focus specifically on gender, rather than custodial status.

10
Nonprofits and For-Profits

A Closer Look

As we have seen, the six for-profit and 20 nonprofit work-first employment programs in New York City use somewhat different practices. On average, for-profits are more focused on quick placement, and they use less job training and case management. Moreover, performance varies by organizational form, with for-profits achieving higher placement rates, on average, and nonprofits having better employment retention rates among those who get jobs. Overall, for-profits have somewhat better results, measured as the share of all participants who get jobs and are still working at any job six months later.

In this chapter we look beyond these comparisons of averages to better understand what makes these nonprofits and for-profits different. With such a small sample size, the findings of this chapter are necessarily suggestive and may not be generalizable to nonprofits and for-profits in general. Even so, New York City is one of only a handful of cities to privatize its employment programs, and it provides a useful opportunity to shed new light on the role of organizational form and performance.

THE DISPERSION OF PRACTICES AND RESULTS BY ORGANIZATIONAL FORM

Comparing the average characteristics of nonprofit and for-profit work-first providers in New York City overlooks a key insight—nonprofits have wider variance in their practices and performance. Some nonprofits strongly encourage participants to consider short-term training while others use no training at all. Likewise, the focus of nonprofits ranges from case management to quick placement. The variance in practices among for-profits, on the other hand, is somewhat smaller. In particular, for-profits are clustered in the midrange to quicker end of the spectrum in terms of placement speeds. (Recall that placement speed is a proxy for the degree to which programs emphasize case management and training.) But they are not, in fact, among the fastest. For example, in terms of median days-to-placement among placed participants, for-profits range from 46 days to 58 days, while nonprofits range from 35 days to 84 days. In terms of training, for-profits range from 0 to 7 percent of participants receiving training vouchers, while nonprofits range from 0 to 14 percent.

The fact that these for-profit programs have less variance in their approaches is consistent with theory. For-profits are thought to have a so-called single-argument objective function. In other words, they have one goal: maximizing profits. If there is a set of profit-maximizing practices, then we would expect to see a convergence around those practices. In contrast, nonprofits are thought to have a two-argument objective function: maximizing profits (or at least breaking even) and "something else" (Needleman 2001). That "something else" often relates to the wishes of its donors. As Moore writes, "In this important sense, there are two bottom lines: mission effectiveness and financial sustainability" (Moore 2000). Given these multiple objectives, it is not surprising that nonprofits have greater willingness to deviate from profit-maximizing practices in the interest of other goals (Weisbroad 1998).

Frumkin and Andre-Clark (2000) describe these dynamics in their examination of welfare-to-work programs:

> [N]onprofits must address the inconsistencies between their values and the quest for short-term and well-defined rules for engagement. Driven by commitments to justice and charity, many nonprofit organizations are consciously oriented away from finding the shortest distance between two points . . . [They] take a more holistic approach to welfare-to-work processes, emphasizing a set of values that providers believe will lead to a better life that are not necessarily closely linked to holding an entry-level job.

In contrast, Frumkin and Andre-Clark argue that for-profit welfare-to-work programs "appear comfortable being tied to the narrowly tailored, short-term goals connected to client employment activity . . . For many for-profits, the shortest distance between welfare receipt and independence from welfare is a straight line through job-related skills and support."

The findings from New York City show that the "something else" part of nonprofits' objective functions—their "mission effectiveness" goal, to use Moore's term—is more important to some organizations than others. At one end of the spectrum, in fact, "something else" approximates "nothing else." These findings imply that what makes nonprofits unique is not a guaranteed commitment to buck the profit motive to achieve their organizational missions, but rather their ability to choose to do so by fundraising, if they wish, to support that choice.

While nonprofits' willingness to deviate from profit-maximizing practices to advance their missions appears to be one factor behind their greater variance in practices, another less benign factor may also be at play—inefficiency. Nonprofits' nondistribution constraint is thought to (beneficially) reduce nonprofit managers' abilities to pursue personal gain or to cut service quality. But Dees and Anderson (2004) remind us that this constraint can also lead to complacency, inefficiency, and waste as they state, "A nonprofit can survive, even thrive, with very inefficient and ineffective practices."

In any case, a "soft and fuzzy" view of nonprofits as necessarily mission driven, or necessarily more empathetic, is certainly not accurate. Some of the 20 nonprofit providers fit those descriptions, but others do not. For example, a director of one of the nonprofit employment programs was asked whether he looks to case managers to help participants deal with more personal barriers to work, such as family problems. His answer was clear, even if a participant were to ask for help in dealing with a sick child:

> Not at all, but they often do it. They often get sucked into it. Even job developers get sucked into that because they get client-oriented rather than employer-orientated. Imagine a private employment agency if somebody said "My kid's sick, what should I do about it?" This is a private employment agency. You're in a shoe store—talk to me about shoes.

Does greater variation in strategies among nonprofits lead to greater variance in results? In terms of placement, it clearly does. Nonprofits' placement rates range from 9 to 26 percent, while for-profits' rates are clustered mostly in the top half, ranging from 18 to 27 percent (Figure 10.1). In terms of overall results, though, for-profits' have only somewhat smaller variance than nonprofits. This is shown in Figure 10.2,

122 Feldman

Figure 10.1 Placement Rates for For-Profit and Nonprofit Programs

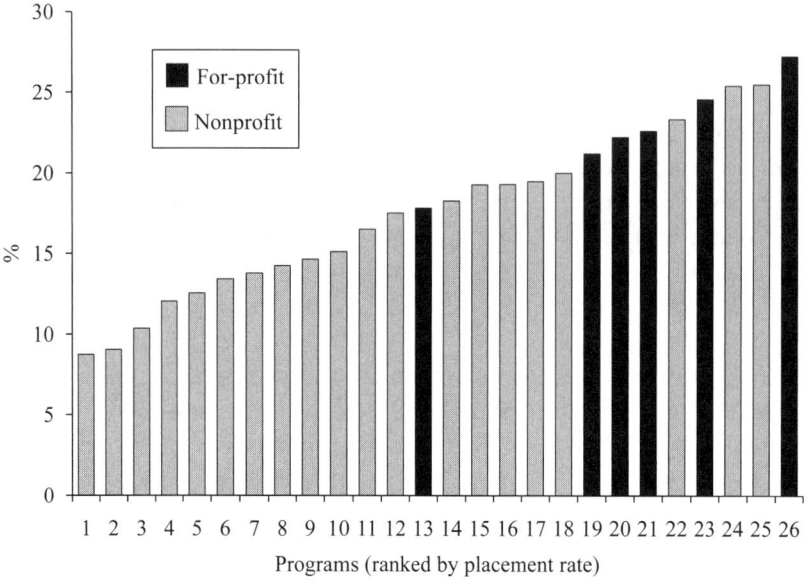

Figure 10.2 Six-Month Caseload Employment Rates for For-Profit and Nonprofit Programs

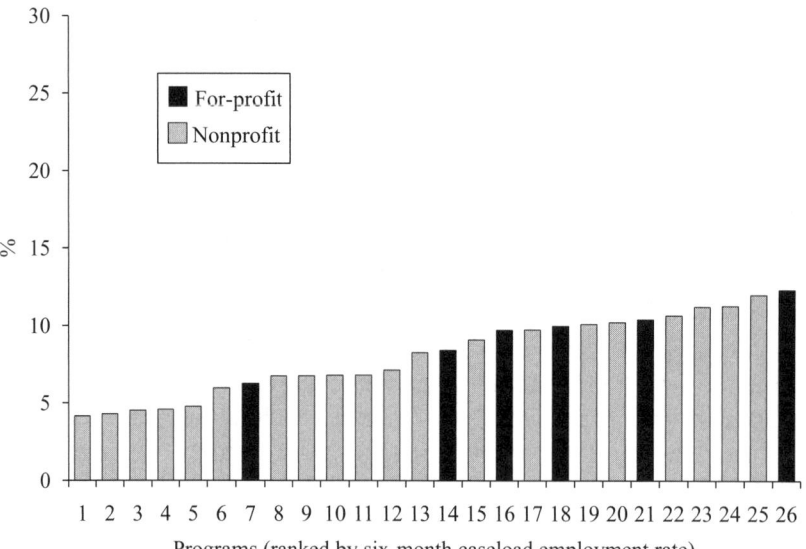

which ranks programs by their six-month caseload employment rate, meaning the share of all participants who get jobs and are still working at any job six months later.

The results of this section suggest that, not surprisingly, for-profits are more responsive to contractual incentives than nonprofits.[1] They also imply that government welfare agencies that design service contracts with for-profits need to be especially careful that the financial incentives are aligned with the results agencies wish to achieve. On the upside, if those agencies are able to specify particular outcomes they wish to maximize, and if they target financial rewards to those outcomes, for-profits should be more responsive than nonprofits to those rewards—in other words, more focused on achieving the desired outcomes.

In the case of New York City, clear outcomes are specified and rewards are targeted to those outcomes via milestone payments. And for-profits do, in fact, achieve those milestones at a higher rate than nonprofits. Of course, from a broader policy perspective, it is a matter of opinion whether for-profits' apparently greater responsiveness to their contracts makes a meaningful difference to performance. Recall that for-profits have a two-percentage-point advantage over nonprofits (10 percent versus 8 percent) in terms of the share of participants that become employed and are still working six months later, a difference of 25 percent. Moreover, the city pays for-profits considerably more, on average, since they achieve 36 percent more total milestones per participant than nonprofits, a result driven by higher placement rates. If one views the performance advantage of for-profits as relatively small, then it appears that the city pays more for for-profit services despite receiving roughly similar results as nonprofits. This would argue for shifting contractual incentives towards six-month employment retention rates and away from more immediate outcomes such as placement. This shift could be justified for a broader reason as well, since both for-profits and nonprofits achieved relatively low levels of sustained employment.

INSIGHTS INTO THE PRACTICE OF CREAMING THE CASELOAD

When welfare-to-work programs focus on the most job-ready individuals, while providing less assistance to harder to serve individuals, it is known as "creaming" or "cream skimming." Creaming is often a concern with welfare-to-work programs, particularly when for-profit providers are involved. For instance, Salamon (1993) argues, "As for-profit firms enter the social market . . . they will inevitably siphon off the more affluent 'customers,' leaving nonprofit firms with the most difficult and least profitable cases." Frumkin and Andre-Clark (2000) add, "many nonprofits—through mission and program design—have demonstrated a special commitment to helping the individual overcome the multiple barriers to employment that many long-term recipients face, [while] business firms have strong incentives to avoid these recipients." Some empirical work from the employment and training literature, however, finds that for-profits do not cream more than nonprofits. Heinrich (2000) examines nonprofit and for-profit contractors in Illinois, operating under the Job Training Partnership Act. Using data from about 750 contracts over a 10-year period, she finds that for-profits are more likely to enroll disadvantaged participants. The results "refute the assertion that nonprofit organizations are inherently more charitable and more likely than for-profit contactors to serve more disadvantaged individuals in delivering publicly funded job-training services."

The outcomes from New York City provide new evidence on the question of whether for-profit service providers engage in creaming to a larger extent than nonprofit ones, particularly under pay-for-performance contracts. The next sections examine the evidence of creaming at three different stages of service delivery: program entry, deassignments and sanctions, and employment services.

Creaming at Program Entry

Because the city randomly assigns welfare recipients to employment programs, those programs cannot "cream" in their original allotment of individuals assigned to them. However, they can try to cream in other ways. For example, programs could attempt to discourage hard-to-serve individuals who are assigned to them from showing up in the first place. They could do this by, say, creating a reputation of being callous to people's problems. Neither fieldwork nor administrative data showed any evidence of this. The 20 nonprofit and six for-profit sites have roughly equal shares of disadvantaged participants (those who show up for at least a day), including the same fraction without a high school degree (45 percent) and with less than a ninth-grade education (6 percent). Both types of programs also have very similar shares of long-term welfare recipients.

Creaming through Deassignments and Sanctions

Once people begin participating, programs have two routes by which they can remove hard-to-serve individuals from their caseloads. First, they can deassign people they categorize as unemployable. Second, they can sanction people for breaking program rules. When someone is deassigned or sanctioned, they are referred back to the city-run Job Centers, and their participation at the employment program ends.

Remarks by a director of a nonprofit program are illustrative of how sanctioning can be used to remove hard-to-serve individuals. He explained that many participants violate at least one rule during their first few days, such as coming in late or not following directions. Most of the time, he said, small infractions are overlooked. But he encourages staff to identify people who are clearly not interested in becoming employed and to sanction them at their first violation. "We're always concerned about diluting staff involvement," he explained, "because even the people who have good prognoses require a lot of service to find a job that's acceptable." He added that every case manager "knows it's in her interest to get rid of the people she doesn't want."[2]

Are for-profit programs in the city more likely to use deassignments or sanctions to cream? The data suggest they are not. For example, Figure 10.3 presents outcomes for the almost 800 long-term custodial welfare recipients in the sample, a population that is particularly challenging to employ and keep employed. Nonprofits deassign at twice the rate of for-profits, and sanctioning rates are quite similar, with for-profits having a slightly higher rate. Comparisons using different definitions of "disadvantaged," including having less than a ninth-grade education, show a similar pattern.

Creaming in Employment Services

Finally, we examine whether for-profits are more likely to cream in their job placement and retention services. The best available test of this is whether hard-to-serve individuals have lower employment outcomes when served by for-profits. The data show, in fact, that for-profit providers achieve somewhat better results than nonprofits for these types of participants. For example, Figure 10.4 shows employment outcomes for long-term welfare recipients. For-profits place a larger share into jobs, and their six-month employment retention rates are identical to nonprofits. As a result, a higher percentage of long-term custodial welfare recipients becomes employed and is still working six months later when served by for-profits (8 percent) than by nonprofits (5 percent).[3] At least among employment programs in New York City, for-profit providers do not appear to engage in creaming to a larger extent than nonprofit providers.

Notes

1. Heinrich (2000) examines Job Training Partnership Act (JTPA) providers and finds no significant differences in the influence of contract performance incentives on outcomes by service provider type. She notes: "This does not imply, however, that the different types of service providers were equally responsive to or likely to satisfy performance requirements." For-profits, in fact, were three times more likely to exceed contract performance standards. While she does not find that for-profits have greater responsiveness to financial incentives in particular, she does find that they have greater responsiveness overall.
2. A legitimate question is whether this type of creaming is an efficient practice from society's point of view. In other words, is it worthwhile to expend limited staff resources on people who, according to staff, do not want jobs? These questions are beyond the scope of this analysis.
3. Results for those with less education show a similar pattern. Moreover, to separate the effects of deassignments and sanctions from placement and retention performance, results were also run using samples that include only participants who were not deassigned or sanctioned. The same overall picture holds.

Figure 10.3 Organizational Practices among For-Profit and Nonprofit Programs for Long-Term Custodial Welfare Recipients

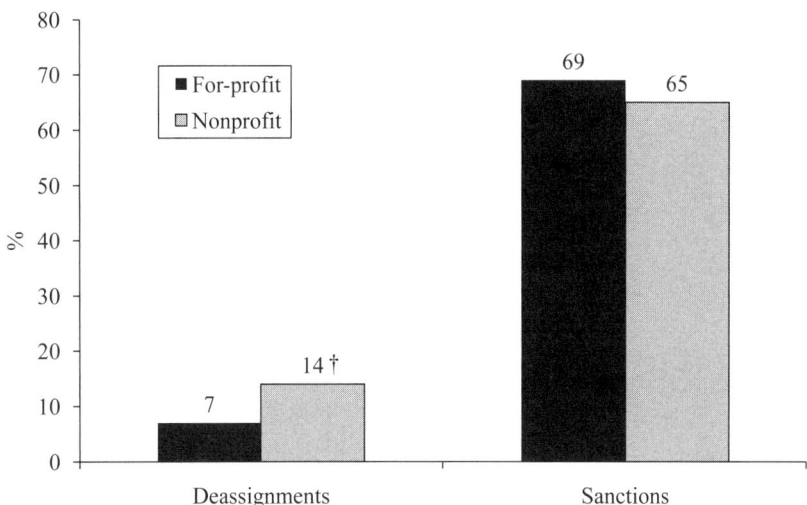

† Difference is statistically significant at the 0.05 level.

Figure 10.4 Employment Outcomes among For-Profit and Nonprofit Programs for Long-Term Custodial Welfare Recipients

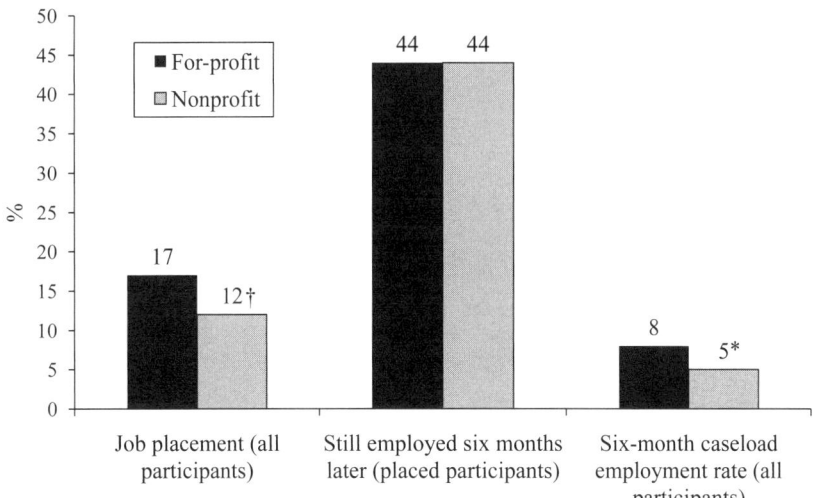

† Difference is statistically significant at the 0.05 level.
* Difference is statistically significant at the 0.10 level.

11
The Role of Management and Leadership

Decisions about which organizational practices to use can significantly affect the performance of work-first employment programs, as we saw in Chapter 9. This fact in itself underscores the importance of management. After all, a key aspect of management (or leadership, if you prefer) is choosing the organization's strategy. In the case of work-first employment services, those choices include whether to emphasize immediate job search or short-term training and whether to take a quick-placement or a case-management approach.

But other, more frontline aspects of management might also be important to performance, such as the ability to establish a clear mission, measure and monitor performance, set organizational goals, and align and motivate staff around those goals. This chapter examines the effect of frontline management practices on welfare-to-work outcomes. The analysis is qualitative—aspects of frontline management are not quantified across programs. Instead, the analysis is more suggestive, drawing on observations from field research as well as programs' outcome data.

HOW MANAGEMENT MATTERS: AN OVERVIEW OF THE LITERATURE

A range of studies demonstrate that public management, defined in a variety of ways, affects the delivery of government services. Brown and Potoski (2006) review the literature and find, "Though a notoriously complex and difficult topic of study, effective management improves government service delivery." Past studies, they note, show a range of managerial tasks and functions that were found to be necessary for successful service delivery, including planning and strategizing, decision-making, budgeting and mobilizing financial resources, managing human resources, evaluating and tracking service quality, and managing across organizational boundaries.

On the other hand, some scholars question how significant a role management plays in service delivery. Looking specifically at welfare-to-work programs, for example, Meyers, Glaser, and MacDonald (1998) find that frontline practices are difficult for management to influence. And Riccucci (2005) writes, "at the front lines of service delivery, where workers may be guided by pervading work norms and customs as well as by shared experiences and knowledge, street-level bureaucrats often perform their job duties and functions while relying very little on management directives." Kettl (2006), commenting on the broader public policy literature, explains that although there is broad agreement among scholars that management matters, some believe that policy matters more. In his words, the latter argument is: "Design the policy well, construct the right incentives, and management will work." Others, he notes, argue that management matters but the odds of successful management are low.

A few studies have examined which frontline management practices matter the most for employment programs. Behn (1991) focuses on Massachusetts' welfare-to-work efforts in the late 1980s and finds that successful program leaders establish a clear mission, set goals for their organizations, personally monitor results, and reward success. Bardach (1993) examines California's Greater Avenues for Independence (GAIN) Program, a statewide welfare-to-work initiative. He argues that useful management practices include delegation of responsibility to line staff; setting measurable, challenging, and fair performance goals; persuading staff that the mission and goals are worthwhile and achievable; and providing proper training to employees.

More recently, Bloom, Hill, and Riccio (2003) pool data from three large-scale experiments to examine the relationship between program implementation and earnings impacts. They find a negative effect of disagreement between staff and supervisors over what a program should be doing or how it should be done. Riccucci (2005) surveys the management literature and finds that job satisfaction is important to organizational outcomes. Her field research in welfare offices also suggests that open communication and participatory management are positively correlated with employees' job satisfaction.

LOOKING ACROSS PROGRAMS

To shed new light onto how management affects the performance of today's work-first employment programs, we turn to the findings from New York City. First, there is no obvious correlation between programs that appear to be better managed and actual participant outcomes. For example, while I was still "blind" to performance (I purposefully had not yet seen programs' performance data), I identified two programs that, based on field research, exemplified strong management capabilities. Both were midsized nonprofits and had directors who were passionate about their work, dedicated to creating high-performance organizations, and thought carefully about how best to keep their staffs motivated. And their staffs did, in fact, appear to be motivated, professional, well trained, and satisfied with their jobs. But as described next, these two programs—referred to here as Sites A and B—achieved quite different employment outcomes. First, though, we take a closer look at the management of each program.

Management at Site A

Site A had a director who showed savvy about organizational design and goal setting. For example, she created teams, each having a case manager, job developer, and retention specialist, and used friendly competition among the teams to spur performance. She avoided setting individual quotas for teams, though, to encourage them to share job leads and useful practices with each other. Moreover, the director closely monitored the program's placement and retention rates, and held weekly staff meetings to review progress and discuss specific cases. "It's not that I want to micromanage the case managers," she explained. "But I also want to make sure that we're thinking about our actions and that we're understanding what the ramifications are. These [participants] are people. They're not a number."

The director also used staff recognition to underscore program goals. For instance, to encourage everyone on the staff to be "placement driven," she awarded certificates to those not part of a team, such as workshop facilitators, who helped the most people find jobs. She also signaled the importance of serving hard-to-employ individuals by awarding vacation days to anyone able to find work for participants she deems especially tough to employ.

Management at Site B

Site B also had a director who was successful at developing a motivated and professional staff. She described her role in creating a positive work environment:

> I'm so lucky and grateful to say I look forward to coming to work. I think if you asked them [the staff] that question, everyone would say that, or at least, the large majority would . . . It's because we work in a very team fashion . . . I so value the staff and they know that. They know that I would back them to the hilt . . . If I'm not supporting them, then they're not going to support the client . . . So it's all modeling and mirroring.

Although she set placement goals for the program, staff motivation also appeared to stem from the director's ability to create a strong sense of mission about serving participants and treating them with respect. Her message to the staff, she explained, was that, "The client's not broken. You don't have to fix them. There's a tremendous amount of strength within each person . . . [The participants] feel that mutual respect." The participants were, in fact, constructively engaged with the staff.

Outcomes at Sites A and B

These two programs were not the only ones with skilled leaders at the helm, but they exemplify thoughtful, participatory leadership focused on creating a culture of performance. Even so, these programs had considerably different results. Figure 11.1 shows the six-month caseload employment rate, meaning the share of participants that are placed in jobs and are still working at any job six months later. Site A had the second-highest rate among the programs, with 12 percent achieving sustained employment. Site B, on the other hand, had a rate that is only half as high (6 percent), placing it sixth from the bottom. When we control for demographic differences, participants were still significantly more likely to achieve six months of employment at Site A than at Site B.

Figure 11.1 Six-Month Caseload Employment Rates

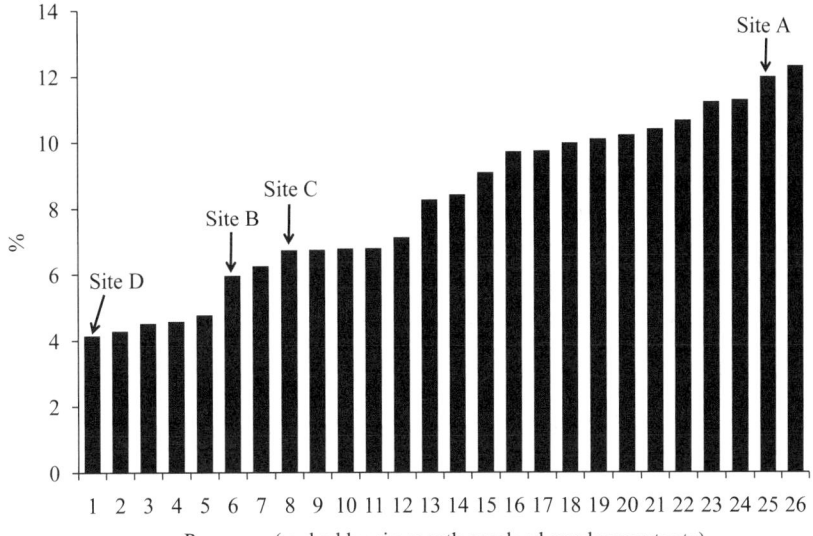

Programs (ranked by six-month caseload employment rate)

Why did these two programs' results differ so much? Although both had capable leaders, the programs used different strategies. The staff at Site A had a clear sense of urgency about getting people into jobs. In fact, a bell rang each time someone got a job, eliciting cheers from the staff and participants. The program was not, in fact, among the fastest in terms of placement speeds (it was the thirteenth fastest), and case management was a valued component of program services. But staff emphasized moving people into jobs with alacrity. Teaming case managers with job developers reflected that emphasis—the purpose of case management was to support and further the goal of speedy placements. Moreover, the level of job training usage at Site A was less than a fourth of that at Site B.

Site B, in contrast, had a goal of teaching people to obtain their own jobs, with guidance from the staff. Only the most job-ready individuals were served by a job developer, while most participants worked in a resource room doing guided job search, or they were referred to training. The staff felt strongly that teaching people to find jobs, or referring them to training, was the most effective way to promote self-sufficiency, rather than finding jobs for people. "Teach a man to fish," as one of the staff put it, referring to the famous parable.

This service strategy, though, resulted in slow placements. Site B ranked last in terms of placement speed, with the median placed participant becoming employed 84 days after program entry, versus 54 days at Site A (thirteenth fastest). That, in turn, meant that people had more time to drop out of the program, and those who stayed likely felt less urgency about becoming employed. As a result, the placement rate of Site B (10 percent) was less than half that of Site A (25 percent). The employment retention rate of placed participants was higher at Site B, an outcome that may be a selection effect, since fewer people got jobs at Site B. Even so, considerably more people became employed and were still working six months later at Site A, as we saw in Figure 11.1.

LOOKING AT PROGRAMS WITH SIMILAR STRATEGIES

The examples of Sites A and B, above, suggest that programs' service strategies are more important to performance than their frontline management practices. Even so, frontline practices do appear to play a noticeable role in determining the outcomes of programs with similar strategies. For example, Sites C and D were similar along several dimensions. Both were nonprofits, had slow placement speeds (the third and fifth slowest, respectively), and encouraged training (the second highest and highest users of training). Although Site D was substantially larger than Site C, both had similar caseload demographics. Yet performance differed between these programs, as shown in Figure 11.1. Site C had a six-month caseload employment rate of almost 7 percent, while Site D had the lowest rate among all programs at about 4 percent, both of which are obviously quite low. Nonetheless, the difference between these rates represents an almost two-thirds advantage for Site C. To explore the possible source of that advantage, we turn to the management of each program.

Management at Site C

Site C had a director that emphasized continually finding ways to improve the program and to keep employees motivated. As he described:

> The biggest challenge is constantly trying to motivate people to function at their highest capacity . . . [and] maintaining a level of excitement and creativity . . . What we try to do is, one, make sure they have the best equipment possible in terms of computers and everything else; their workspace is as good as it can possibly be; we try to give them as much autonomy as we can to make decisions on their own; . . . try to be flexible in terms of time and leave.

The way he managed, he explained, was "participatory, democratic," but with close oversight of the program: "You give people as much decision-making capabilities as you possibly can. You have them check in. For instance, everybody feeds me information. When we have a new group coming in, I get the test results. Whenever we make a submission to HRA [to be paid by the city] for placements, I get those results." His efforts to make the workplace a positive environment included small gestures, such as allowing employees to listen to music at their desks. Fieldwork showed that staff did, in fact, enjoy their jobs and worked cooperatively together.

Management at Site D

The situation at Site D was quite different. Staff generally felt unappreciated and many were dissatisfied with their jobs. As a job developer explained, speaking about the program's leaders:

> [T]hey're on you about quotas; they're on you about time sheets; they're on you if you're 15 minutes late when you sign in . . . they put a yellow line by your name which means you're late . . . [Employees] are not happy . . . They feel underpaid . . . So there's no real motivation because they are busting their butts and not being compensated for the work. Where's the motivation to come to work and smile?

Employees' dissatisfaction also stemmed from a lack of cooperation between the staff, particularly between case managers and job developers. From the view of case managers (as one explained), job developers "usually blame the case managers for everything . . . It's supposed to be a cohesive effort, but it's not." The fact that this case manager felt no responsibility for making placements (he stated, "I have nothing to do with job development") highlights the gulf between these two types of staff.

Moreover, conflict within this program also occurred among job developers. Pressure to meet placement quotas set by management was intense, a job developer explained, calling the quotas "unfair." Because of the pressure, some job developers "hoarded" participants, not allowing them to work with other job developers. This, not surprisingly, led to conflict among job developers.

Finally, Site D was struggling with disorganization. As a result of recent program modifications, staff members were not always sure where they should be or what they should be doing. At one workshop I attended, no staff members showed up for the first 45 minutes, leaving participants sitting in a classroom, visibly frustrated.

Despite this program's problems, the director appeared smart and personable, and had many years of management experience. But her comments showed less emphasis on motivating and monitoring the staff than those of Site C's director. When asked to describe her role, for example, she noted that she was frequently at meetings away from the office: "I have a deputy director here who oversees the day-to-day."

While the director set placement quotas for job developers, case managers "don't really have any goals" set by management, she noted. She also explained that case managers had up to 100 people on their caseloads, acknowledging, "You cannot case manage a hundred people—it's not going to happen." Finally, she spoke about her frustration with the staff and blamed them for high dropout rates:

> This has been a bone of contention . . . to get the staff to understand what needs to be done. And I'm saying "If you're not on task and not on board, don't expect the customer to be. And when you go to class [i.e., teach a workshop] you start with 30 people and you only end up with 10 [at the end of the two weeks], why is that? It's not the customer's fault. It's your fault. Because they showed up.

Given the tension between management and staff, and among the staff, it is not surprising that turnover was high, according to interviewees.[1]

Outcomes at Sites C and D

Surprisingly, placement rates were actually slightly higher at Site D (13 percent) than at Site C (12 percent). The employment retention rate, on the other hand, was much lower at Site D. Only a third of those placed in jobs are still working six months later, compared to more than half at Site C. As a result, the six-month caseload employment rate is higher at Site C, as shown in Figure 11.1.

Did the lack of job satisfaction and teamwork at Site D lead to its worse overall performance? It may have, even though placement rates were similar at both programs. Job developers at Site D were still able to place people into jobs despite not working productively with case managers and having low morale. But without the cooperation of case managers to get people job ready, it appears that retention rates suffered. In addition, retention services may have been inadequate at Site D. The director noted, in fact, that she set goals for her retention staff related to three-month retention rates but not to six-month rates. Not surprisingly, there was a large drop in employment retention at Site D between three and six months after placement. The type of goals set, in other words, is another area of frontline management that apparently affected performance.

THE IMPORTANCE OF AN EFFECTIVE STRATEGY

The examples of Sites C and D demonstrate that two programs with similar program strategies (a case-management focus and an emphasis on short-term job training) can produce somewhat different results, with management practices appearing to play a role. But the more definitive finding is that organizational strategy is a more powerful determinant of outcomes than frontline management. As we saw with Sites A and B, employing a quick-placement focus rather than a case-management focus and requiring immediate job search rather than encouraging training were decisions that had much more obvious consequences to performance than whether managers were able to develop a motivated and cohesive staff.

Further evidence on this point is shown in Figure 11.2. Like the previous figure, it shows the share of participants who become employed and are still working six months later. Gray-shaded bars signify programs that refer at least 5 percent of their participants to training or have slow placement speeds (an indicator of a case-management focus), but not both. Black bars, on the other hand, indicate programs that fit both these categories, encouraging training and having slow placement

Figure 11.2 Six-Month Caseload Employment Rates: Results for Programs with Slow Placement Speeds and/or That Encourage Job Training

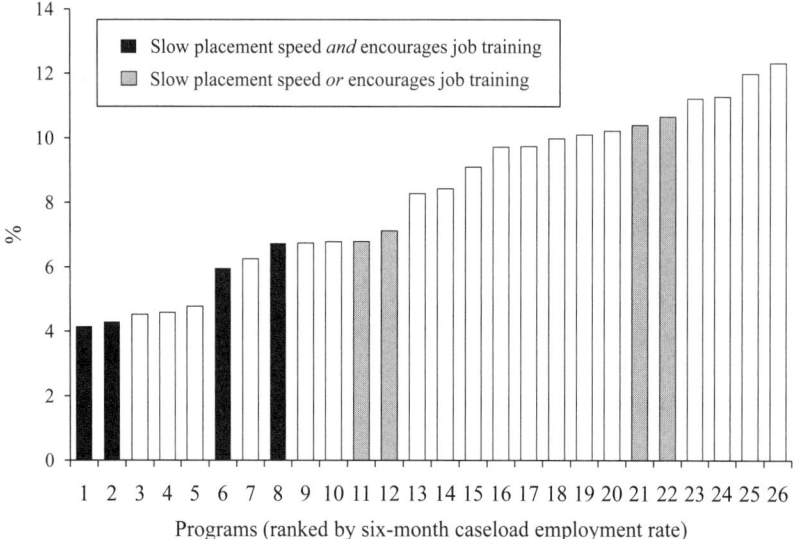

speeds. The figure shows that only two of the four programs that emphasize case management or encourage training (the gray bars) are in the top half of performance, while none of the four programs that do both is in the top half (the black bars). To a large extent, therefore, strategy is destiny. Even programs with insightful, dedicated leaders and motivated staff are constrained from being top performers if they implement a less effective strategy—in this case, emphasizing both case management and the type of short-term, classroom based training used in New York City. So why would employment service providers use these types of less effective practices? The next chapter investigates that question.

Note

1. This program leader, and others interviewed, had control over the hiring process. So a lack of autonomy in hiring did not appear to be an issue.

12
Why Programs Choose Suboptimal Practices

The findings from New York City suggest that the service strategies of work-first employment programs have important consequences on their outcomes. For example, as shown in Chapter 9, the estimated combined effect of using less short-term job training, becoming more focused on quick placement, and moving from partial to full performance-based pay is to more than double the share of participants that achieve at least six months of employment. Yet many programs do not use these "better practices," choosing instead to implement—and to continue using—less effective or "sub-optimal" ones. This chapter discusses four possible explanations for why certain programs use suboptimal practices. The explanations are not mutually exclusive, so a combination of factors may be at play for some programs.

IMPERFECT INFORMATION

Which specific practices within work first are effective is a subject that has not been well studied. It is not surprising, then, that program leaders sometimes use practices that they believe are effective, but about which they have little hard evidence. For example, one nonprofit director wondered out loud about whether his program would have better results if it were more focused on quick placement, with more pressure on job developers to place people in jobs, "Do those job developers that are driven by absolute outcomes and quotas, do a better job? I don't know the answer to that, but it would be interesting [to find out]."

In terms of accessible information about whether certain programs are performing better or worse than others—data that can help program leaders decide if different practices are needed—New York City provides a uniquely large amount of information. Every month, the city's HRA creates "VendorStat" reports for all 26 programs. Each report contains data on 20 performance measures for each program, as well as program rankings on those measures and citywide averages. The data allow program leaders to gauge their relative performance in terms of job placement, employment retention, and other measures.

Even with these data, though, determining causal linkages between specific practices and outcomes is not easy. Moreover, program leaders typically do not know what practices other programs are using—information that could help illuminate those causal linkages. Programs that run multiple sites, or that are in coalitions such as the EarnFair Alliance, would presumably have an advantage in terms of sharing "what works." But the data show no evident advantages from these relationships. In fact, EarnFair Alliance programs underperform as compared with other programs, despite the fact that they have regular meetings in which staff from different programs discuss their practices and share advice.

MAXIMIZING ALTERNATIVE DEFINITIONS OF PERFORMANCE

Another potential reason that some employment programs achieve fewer placement and retention milestones (the achievements on which programs' compensation is based) is that some programs may not, in fact, be trying to maximize those milestones. The clearest examples within New York City's system are programs that reject the "any job is better than no job" philosophy. They emphasize case management and job-readiness assistance, including job training in some cases, and are reluctant to put pressure on participants to accept jobs. Their intent, it appears, is to maximize people's well-being (with a still-evident emphasis on placement into jobs) as opposed to the more common focus among programs of maximizing placement into jobs (with a still-evident emphasis on improving people's well-being).

A specific example is a small community-based program, part of the EarnFair Alliance, that was committed to case management and to giving people enough time to become work ready. That commitment, the director explained, does not help the program financially, since "we aren't focusing on the numbers, [but] if we don't perform on the basis of the contract, we don't get paid." For instance, the program's placement philosophy was to find people jobs that were "desirable for them" rather than saying "we need to get this placement no matter what." The program ranked 19 out of 26 in terms of placement, although its retention rates among placed participants was above average (eleventh). Overall, it ranked fifteenth in terms of the share of participants who got jobs and were still working after six months. The organization was losing money on the contract with the city, but it was willing to fundraise to cover costs and maintain its service strategy.

Contrast that example with another program, a for-profit, which clearly had maximizing contractual milestones as its goal. One of the job developers, for example, explained how their focus was on "sales," meaning pitching participants to employers and pitching jobs to participants, rather than on case management: "We have an emphasis on doing the sales. Plus, we have a social conscience. They [nonprofits] are the reverse: They have the social conscience, then the sales thing comes afterwards." Fieldwork shows that for-profit programs in New York City are somewhat more focused on quick placement than case management, on average. Nonprofits, on the other hand, span a wider spectrum, from placement driven to case-management focused. The main point here, though, is that different definitions of "performance" and "success" help explain why programs use different practices.

COMPETENCY TRAPS

A "competency trap" exists when organizations become skilled at doing certain things and, as a result, face disincentives towards searching for better ways of operating (March 1994). For example, several employment programs in New York City have been using job training for years, either providing it themselves or referring people to external providers. Over time, program leaders and staff presumably gained confidence in their abilities to use training effectively. Shifting away from training would entail several possible costs, including developing new practices and staffing capabilities, and severing relationships with training providers. In fact, formerly training-focused programs might need to develop a whole new organizational culture. These types of costs can create competency traps, inducing organizations to stick with their current practices, even if those practices are less effective.

A similar competency trap could occur for programs with a case-management approach. Leaders at these programs tend to have backgrounds in social work and feel personally committed to providing quality job-readiness assistance. Shifting to a quick-placement approach would involve not only staff retooling, but uprooting practices that may be central to employees' conceptions of what it means to serve the jobless and the poor. The latter factor also relates to another type of trap, the identity trap, which is discussed next.

IDENTITY TRAPS

An "identity trap" occurs when an organization is unable to adapt to changes in its environment because the change would be inconsistent with its core identity (Bouchikhi and Kimberly 2003). For example, program leaders who see their organizations as social-service agencies might find it difficult to adopt a quick-placement approach that provides only light case management. Another example involves the three employment programs in New York City run by community colleges. The mission of these colleges is to provide education and training, so it is not surprising that they designed their welfare-to-work programs to emphasize skill building. Each program sends an above-average level of participants to job training. In fact, staff members at these three programs even call their participants "students," underscoring the link with their educational settings. Switching to a quick-placement approach, with little training usage, would be difficult for these programs.

Fieldwork suggests that all four of the potential explanations, discussed above, play a role in explaining why some programs use suboptimal practices. An implication is that simply attributing less effective practices to "managerial incompetence" overlooks factors that can have a quite rational basis. Those factors include the costs of changing practices and the fact that some organizations are trying to maximize different outcomes. Even with perfect information, therefore, we might not see similar practices across programs. Nonetheless, hard evidence about the effects of various practices on outcomes can help programs make better decisions about their service strategies, and help government lawmakers and administrators make better decisions about policy design and implementation.

THE NEED FOR INNOVATION

Leaders of work-first programs can improve their organizations' performance by being alert to competency and identity traps, and by dealing with imperfect information by seeking out or generating evidence about what works.[1] The goal of this book is provide that type of new evidence. The unique characteristics of New York City's welfare system, and its sample size of 26 programs, mean that the findings may or may not be applicable elsewhere. Even so, New York City's experience provides several interesting insights and hypotheses for further research. In particular, the data suggest that programs have better employment outcomes when they offer a quick route into employment, rather than emphasizing short-term classroom-based job training, more intensive case management, or both. Programs with stronger performance incentives also have better outcomes, according to the data.

Yet the broader and most startling finding, or reminder, of the book is the stark challenge of helping welfare recipients become and stay employed. Of the 20,677 individuals referred to the city's employment programs during the sample period in the mid 2000s, only 6 percent became employed and was still working at any job six months later. New York City's relatively lenient sanction policies are likely an important factor behind this result, given the widespread noncompliance within the system. But more effective employment programs and policies are clearly needed as well. As a start, if all of the employment programs in New York City used the "better practices" discussed in the previous chapters, including having a quick-placement focus and fully performance-based contracts, the data suggest that the percentage of participants that would get jobs and would still be working six months later could reach almost 14 percent, more than double the current rate. This would be an important achievement, with thousands of additional participants connected to employment each year.

These findings underscore the need in New York City, and across the nation, for innovations that can significantly boost the employment success of welfare recipients and other low-income Americans. Innovations might relate to employment strategies, such as increased financial rewards to work or restructured public service jobs. They might relate to skill-building strategies, such as different ways of integrating work, education, and job training, or new ways of tying training to in-demand jobs. Or they might relate to job-retention strategies, such as more effective forms of postplacement follow-up and coaching or new partnerships between programs and employers. Significant advancements will require fresh ideas combined with opportunities to rigorously test and evaluate them. A better understanding of today's work-first programs and their results is a building block for that innovation.

Note

1. Ways that leaders can generate new evidence about what works include implementing new practices and seeing if they affect performance, or comparing their programs' performance to other programs and investigating what organizational differences may be driving different outcomes.

Appendix A
Methodology

I conducted this study as a performance analysis, meaning my aim was to not only describe how organizations implement their programs, but also to relate those practices to measures of performance (Mead 2003). First, I undertook exploratory fieldwork to form hypotheses about what affects performance, conducting full-day site visits at 20 of the 26 sites during November 2004 through March 2005. Sites were chosen with input from New York City's HRA to include a range of organizational sizes and types, as well as high, average, and low performers in terms of placement and retention. I conducted the site visits "blind" to performance, meaning that I did not know the programs' performance levels, to allow for the formation of unbiased hypotheses.[1] Organizational characteristics were identified that represented the clearest differences among programs.

Interviews were semistructured (Weiss 1994), which allowed me to discuss new or unexpected determinants of program performance. An interview protocol was created based on topics investigated by past studies of welfare-to-work programs (Behn 1991; Bardach, 1993; Bloom and Michalopoulos, 2001; Bloom, Hill, and Riccio, 2003). It covered issues relating to organizational strategy, current operations, and the use of specific practices.

CHARACTERIZING SITE-LEVEL PRACTICES

Performance analyses require quantitatively characterizing the organizational characteristics at each program. For some variables, administrative data exist, including deassignment rates, referrals to sanctions, and program size. Programs' use of training is measured by the percentage of participants at each program that receive training vouchers. To measure the degree to which programs use a quick-placement approach versus a case-management approach, average placement speed is used, which is measured as the number of days it takes a program to place the median participant among placed participants only. It is assumed that programs with faster placement speeds have greater urgency about getting people employed, whereas those with slower speeds have a greater focus on case management and other job-readiness activities.[2] These assumptions are supported by fieldwork. Site visits and interviews suggest a strong connection between programs' focus on quick placement versus case management and their placement speeds. An example is the program mentioned in Chapter 7 whose director had redesigned his program to emphasize quick placement, cutting the time participants spent in workshops and having people meet with job developers more quickly. This site had the third fastest placement speed, with a median of 42 days to placement.

As an example from the other end of the spectrum, staff at the program with the second-slowest placement speed (83 days to placement) had a strong commitment to helping people become job ready and not to "push" anyone into a job.[3] Staff characterized themselves as not "numbers focused," and the director said that making good job matches was more important than achieving placement milestones. Programs with moderate placement speeds typically display a mixed approach, with case managers playing an important role, but staff having a sense of urgency about placement.

Evidence that placement speed is linked to programs' sense of urgency about placement and level of emphasis on barrier removal is also supported by the fact that other potential influences of placement speeds do not appear to play significant roles. First, the number of job developers relative to program size has no statistically significant correlation with placement speed or performance, making it unlikely that staff capacity, rather than staff actions, drives the connection between placement speeds and performance. Second, the use of random assignment within boroughs for most individuals means that unmeasured demographic characteristics are less likely to influence placement speed differences. Between boroughs, average placement speeds differ modestly. Finally, fieldwork did not suggest a connection between a longer time to placement and staff incompetence.

A legitimate concern with using placement speed as a variable is that it is partially endogenous. The fact that the variable is constructed based on the outcomes of placed participants only, rather than all participants, helps limit endogeneity. Moreover, when this variable is removed from the regression models presented below, results are similar.[4]

DEFINING THE SAMPLE

At the organizational level, the sample includes all 26 programs. The analysis focuses on programs rather than the 19 providers (some providers run more than one program). Although programs run by the same firms implemented roughly similar strategies, program leaders had discretion in choosing operational emphases. In fact, staff who had worked at more than one program run by the same company or provider noted differences in the ways they were run. Because organizational-level variables are of primary interest here, the effective number of observations in this study is the number of programs, not the number of participants. However, having individual-level demographic data on participants allowed a more accurate account of variation in the populations across programs.

An important methodological decision is how to define the sample at the individual level. The main definition used here is all individuals assigned to programs during the sample period who showed up for at least one day, a group that is termed "participants." Other individual-level sample definitions are possible as well, including all individuals referred to programs (whether or not they showed up). Results based on alternative samples tell a similar story of "what works," showing that the sample definition does not drive the findings.

INVESTIGATING EFFECTIVE PRACTICES

To investigate effective practices among programs, logistic regressions are used based on data on all individuals who entered programs during the five months of fieldwork. In particular, the results in Chapter 9 are based on multilevel logistic regressions, which account for the nested structure of the data, where sample members (level 1) are grouped by programs (level 2). As a result, a two-level hierarchal model is estimated (Raudenbuch and Bryk 2002), which is similar to the methodology used by Bloom, Hill, and Riccio (2003). The purpose of using a multilevel model is to produce unbiased estimators for level 2 because research has demonstrated bias with models using ordinary least squares (OLS). The model, which also produces more efficient estimates in a multilevel setting than OLS, is shown in Figure A.1. Explanatory variables at the organizational level (O) relate to program practices and characteristics.[5]

The purpose of the model is to test how programs' organizational characteristics affect performance, focusing on characteristics where programs differ most markedly. Because the program-level sample size is 26, a limited number of characteristics can be tested. Therefore, variables are excluded from the models where two conditions are met: 1) field research did not suggest that the characteristic has an important influence on performance, and 2) correlations show few or no significant relationships with performance.[6] Excluded variables are program size, sanction rate, and whether or not a program is faith based.

Figure A.1 Multilevel Model of Participant Outcomes

Level 1 (individual-level submodel)

$P = \alpha + \gamma D + \Psi L + \varepsilon$,

where P = binary measure representing if the participant became employed or not (or, for other models, whether they became employed and were still working three or six months later)
α = intercept
D = vector of individual-level demographic controls
L = vector of borough fixed effects
γ, Ψ = vectors of regression coefficients
ε_1 = error term

Level 2 (program-level submodel)

$\alpha = \lambda + \beta O + \varepsilon$,

where α = intercept from the individual-level submodel
λ = intercept
O = vector of organizational variables (measured at the site level) related to ESP practices
β = a vector of regression coefficients
ε_2 = error term

Full model

$P = (\lambda + \beta O + \varepsilon_2) + \gamma D + \varepsilon_1 \rightarrow P = \lambda + \beta O + \gamma D + \varepsilon_3$

NOTE: The model is based on a logit transformation of the expected probability, and the distribution of the error term is logistic.

SAMPLE MEANS

Variables related to the five characteristics where programs differ are included in the model: for-profit status, EarnFair Alliance membership, de-assignment rate, share of participants referred to training, and length of time to median placement among placed individuals.[7] Five organizational-level variables was considered to be a judicious number because the variables' standard errors do not increase significantly (and often continue to decrease) when each variable is added to the model. The regression models use several definitions of performance, and the dependent variable is specified at the individual level. Even so, the relevant sample size remains at the program level (26) because organizational variables are of primary interest.

Table A.1 provides overview statistics for the five program-level variables, and Table A.2 does the same for the demographic variables included in the regression models. The latter table includes data on the national TANF caseload during the study period (mid 2000s) for comparison. Since all TANF recipients are custodial parents, national data should be compared with the column for custodial participants in New York City. Also note that the city has a much larger share of long-term recipients than the national average. One reason is because of New York State's more lenient welfare rules, but another, probably more important factor, is that long-term recipients in New York City are concentrated in these 26 programs. Recall that new recipients are served by another set of programs. The sample is also somewhat older and has a much larger share of black non-Hispanic recipients than the national TANF caseload.

THE USE OF RANDOM ASSIGNMENT

Most previous nonexperimental studies of welfare-to-work program performance have two methodological challenges. First, clients self-select which program in which participate, and this selection is, presumably, at least partially based on unobservable characteristics that cannot be accounted for in the analysis. Second, program characteristics are not assigned randomly to sites, complicating researchers' abilities to compare program performance. The methodology of this study largely solves the first challenge (but not perfectly, given that anecdotal evidence indicates that participants are sometimes able to request assignments to particular programs). While this is an important improvement over most of the literature, it is important to note that the second challenge remains. Because program characteristics are not assigned randomly to sites, there may be unobservable factors that influence program performance that could bias the results. Overcoming this limitation would require programs

Table A.1 Program Characteristics

	Mean	Min	Max
Program size (per new class)	50	14	174
Deassignment rate (%)	13	5	42
Sanction rate (%)	55	36	75
Training referrals (%)	3	0	16
Length of time to median placement (among placed)	56 days	35 days	84 days
Sample size		26 programs	

Table A.2 Participant Characteristics (%)

	Study sample			National data
	Full sample	Noncustodial individuals	Custodial individuals	U.S. TANF caseload
12+ years of education	54.9	58.1	52.6	58.6
Long-term recipient[a]	31.0	11.6	45.3	4.9
Male	30.9	58.0	10.9	9.4
< 20 years old	2.5	1.9	3.0	7.4
20–29 years old	31.0	17.8	40.7	47.6
30–39 years old	28.1	21.2	33.4	28.2
40 or older	38.4	59.2	22.9	16.8
0 custodial children	42.4	100.0	0.0	0.0
1 custodial child	25.4	0.0	44.1	48.9
2 custodial children	17.5	0.0	30.5	27.7
3+ custodial children	5.9	0.0	25.4	21.6
Black, non-Hispanic	64.6	66.7	62.9	38.9
White, non-Hispanic	5.2	6.8	4.0	36.7
Hispanic	30.3	26.9	32.9	19.1
Asian	0.7	0.7	0.6	1.5
Other	1.7	1.6	1.7	3.9
Sample size	14,079	5,995	8,103	2,113,090

NOTE: The sample is individuals who were assigned to programs between November 2004 and March 2005 and who showed up for at least a day. Data for U.S. averages relate to adult TANF recipients and are from *Characteristics and Financial Circumstances of TANF Recipients, FY 2004* (U.S. Department of Health and Human Services 2006).

[a] Data from New York City on the exact amount of time on welfare (lifetime or current cycle) are not available. However, data do exist on whether custodial parents have been on welfare for five or more years during their lifetimes, and whether noncustodial parents have been on welfare for two or more years during their lifetimes. Therefore, the definition of "long-term receipt" varies between these two groups.

to be randomly assigned a "style" of operating—for example, how much job training and case management to provide.

In terms of the extent to which assignments are random, one way to investigate this issue is to compare participants' demographic characteristics at different programs. For example, a comparison of the distribution of long-term welfare recipients by program shows considerable variation in Manhattan and Queens, and somewhat less variation in Brooklyn and the Bronx. Statistical tests (F-tests) indicate that there is statistically significant variation between sites within most boroughs in terms of the share of long-term recipients. Statistically significant differences also exist among the boroughs in terms of the share of participants with less than 12 years of education. These findings suggest that nonrandom assignments occur, to some extent, in all of the boroughs. Although consistent random assignment would be ideal, most performance analyses of welfare-to-work programs do not have even partial random assignment, so this feature of New York City's welfare system remains valuable to the study. Moreover, individual-level controls on a range of demographic variables are available, and were used in the quantitative analysis presented in Chapter 9, to control for observable caseload differences.

Notes

1. Those hypotheses turned out to be mostly incorrect. I predicted, based on my field research, that programs that provided more case management and more referrals to job training would do better, although the results suggest the opposite. This underscores the value of using both qualitative and quantitative research elements. Quantitative performance data allowed me to test my hypotheses, while qualitative research helped me frame the questions and to better interpret and understand the results. Hollister (2008), commenting on an earlier version of this book, writes: "Here is an example of 'mixed methods' capitalizing on the necessity to allocate scarce 'slots' in programs [by employing random assignment] to obtain a causal inference, and at the same time see how well a priori assessment of likely 'performance' predicts the actual impacts."
2. Since training also slows placement speeds, the speed-to-placement variable indicates a quick-placement versus a case-management approach with training held constant in the econometric models.
3. The program with the overall slowest speed is not used as an example because it emphasized training as well as teaching people how to find their own jobs (something unique to this site). This contributed to its slow speed regardless of the level of case management provided.
4. The only noteworthy change caused by removing the "placement speed" variable is that the effect of training becomes larger because programs that encourage training have slower average placements.
5. Although a three-level model could be used to reflect the fact that participants are grouped within offices that are grouped within boroughs, for simplification, borough dummy variables are included in level 1 of a two-level model instead. This may produce inaccurate standard errors for the borough fixed effects, but this is not critical to the analysis.
6. This semiexploratory approach is also used because making a priori predications about the connection between program characteristics and performance is difficult.

7. A related methodological issue is the "bundling" of these organizational characteristics—that is, the degree to which programs display useful variation in terms of those characteristics. For simplicity, we can think of all five variables as binary by characterizing the continuous variables as either high or low values. Doing so would allow for 24 possible combinations of operating styles. One style, for example, is: for-profit, non-EarnFair, low deassignment rate, low use of training, and quick placement speed. It could be, moreover, that programs come in only a handful of operating styles. If that were true, it would be harder to distinguish which characteristics are important. It would also be more difficult to assume that program managers could adjust one variable while holding other variables constant. But the data show this is not the case. Sites come in a relatively wide variety of operating styles. Among the 24 possible operating styles, 17 are represented by different programs. This variation increases our ability to measure which characteristics and practices are most important for performance and also makes it more realistic to assume that managers can adjust individual program practices.

Appendix B
Using Guided Job Search

Although most programs use job developers as the primary method of connecting participants with jobs, some also encourage participants to search for their own jobs, while assisting and monitoring them in the process. This supervised approach to job search is called "guided job search" to differentiate it from the more traditional "independent job search," where people spend time job searching on their own, with little supervision.

At a fairly large program, for example, participants who are not meeting individually with their job developers meet in a resource room where another job developer teaches them how to conduct their own job searches. "The way the job development network rooms are set up is to get maximum efficiency in the time that they have here," the director explained. "Each room has five computers with internet access, fax machine, three phones, and a job developer fully engaged with them."

Interestingly, none of the programs in New York City uses independent job search.[1] As a case manager explained, "If they were able to do independent job search, there would be no reason for them to be referred to our program." A job developer at a different program explained how she had been able to fake independent job search as a welfare recipient, years ago:

> In here there's no independent job search. As a former welfare recipient, that's all I did . . . They said "Go ahead, do your job search and bring back business cards [as proof]." For one day, I just walked all over and got about 50 business cards and then stayed out for three or four days [and then said] "Here—this is where I was." They allowed that to happen.

One reason programs today are able to avoid using independent job search is the Internet, which enables participants to search for jobs without physically leaving the site, enabling staff to directly monitor and assist their efforts.

RATIONALE FOR USING GUIDED JOB SEARCH

Staff members at programs that use guided job search (usually as a supplement to the work of job developers) cite several reasons for doing so. One is that job development staff can only meet with so many participants at a time.

When participants are not meeting with job developers or are not in workshops, guided job search can keep people busy and, hopefully, lead to some job placements.

Others encourage guided job search as a way to reduce a mindset of dependency by having people take partial responsibility for finding jobs. In the words of one job developer, who was also a former welfare recipient:

> Public assistance allows people to [be dependent] . . . Someone's paying your rent, medical, food stamp, giving you a little chump change. Before the end of the month, you're broke and you're waiting for that check . . . So when you come here [you might say] "Now give me a job!" [But I say:] "No, my job is not to give you a job. My job is to show you how to find a job so you won't ever be in this position again."

A third rationale is based on the belief that guided job search leads to higher rates of job retention and less welfare recidivism. "Because they learned how to [find jobs] themselves—they got the job they wanted ... they'll stay at that job," a job developer explained. "And they'll know that, 'Even if I don't want to stay here [in the current job], I can always go find my own job. I don't have to come back within the system.'"

GUIDED JOB SEARCH AS A PRIMARY TOOL

Only one program uses guided job search as the primary way in which participants are connected with jobs. There, all but the most job-ready individuals (who meet directly with the job developer) are taught how to find their own jobs, rather than being referred to interviews by a job developer. The process begins by having case managers meet one on one with participants to discuss employment fields they wish to pursue. They then discuss specific jobs that would be appropriate based on their skills, interests, and salary goals. Next, participants investigate job opportunities in a computer resource room where staff teach people how to set up free e-mail accounts, create resumes, use on-line job-search programs such as Monster.com, and write cover letters. Before going on job interviews, participants meet with the job developer to do practice interviews. One staff member characterized the process as "self-empowerment."

ARGUMENTS AGAINST GUIDED JOB SEARCH

Staff members at most other programs see the use of job developers as more effective than guided job search. In particular, they cited the motivating nature of going on job interviews quickly after program entry, without having to wait to learn job-search techniques. Moreover, quality control is easier, they said, when job developers have the primary responsibility for finding jobs. "When people find their own jobs, it can be a job that's off the books, it's a job without benefits, there are all kind of problems that come up," explained Susan Meloccaro, President of the for-profit Career and Education Consultants. Others noted that tapping into job developers' knowledge of employers was valuable, especially in terms of knowing the types of skills particular employers are looking for, and what types of work environments those employers provide. A job developer's comments underscore this point:

> An HR person [at a business], if they put an ad in the paper, they're looking at a hundred resumes a day. My job is to get my person an interview . . . [And] I don't want to have people just walking around going on interviews without getting a job. The reality is that they're on public assistance. They need to get jobs. It's very frustrating being on public assistance. It's very frustrating going on interviews without getting hired.

IS GUIDED JOB SEARCH MORE EFFECTIVE?

Do programs that use guided job search produce better results than those that rely only on job developers? One way to investigate this question is by comparing the results of the site that uses guided job search as a primary job-matching method (call it Program G) with the average of the other 25 programs. As Figure B.1 shows, the placement rate at Program G (10 percent) is substantially below that of other programs (18 percent). In fact, it is the third-lowest placement rate among the programs. On the other hand, the share of placed participants that received higher wage jobs (43 percent) is the highest among all programs and is more than double the average for the other programs (20 percent). The third set of columns shows that the employment retention rate among placed participants is also much higher at Program G, ranking it second among the programs.

The results suggest that a guided job-search model can connect placed participants with higher quality jobs and produce better employment retention

Figure B.1 Guided Job Search as a Primary Job-Matching Tool

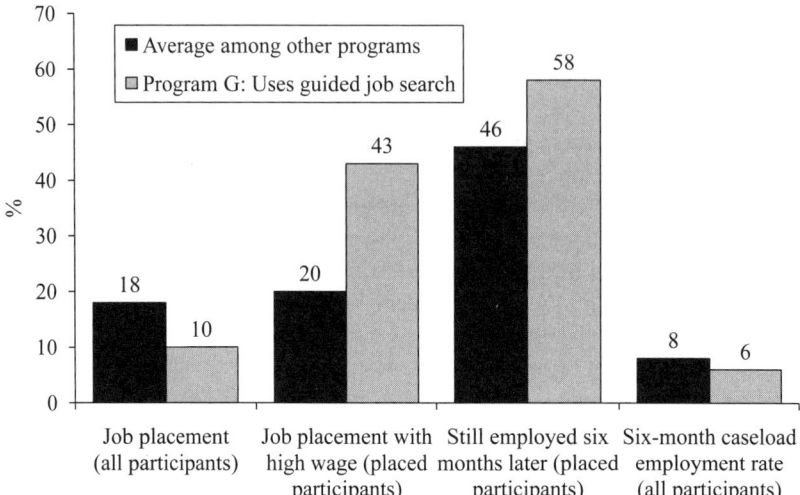

rates. Yet this likely reflects, at least in part, a selection effect. Fewer people become employed at this program, so those who are placed are likely to be more advantaged, with higher wages and better employment retention regardless of the program. Data on participant demographics confirm that placed participants at Program G are more likely to have a high school degree and are less likely to be a long-term welfare recipient as compared to the average placed participant at other programs.

Finally, as a result of this program's low placement rate, fewer participants actually become employed and keep working for at least six months. Six percent of all participants achieved at least six months of employment at Program G, as compared with 8 percent at other programs, on average. Although these findings are based on only one program that uses guided job search as its primary job-placement strategy, they provide preliminary evidence that this strategy does not produce better results for a broad range of welfare recipients than a job-developer-driven approach.

Note

1. Research has shown that independent job search is not the most effective method of helping welfare recipients find employment. For example, Sandfort (2000), using data from Michigan, finds that independent job search has no effect on the proportion of a county's welfare caseload that finds employment.

Appendix C
Chapter 9 Regression Results

This appendix presents regression results for custodial participants because these results are the most relevant to national policy. The regression tables show marginal effects for the modal (that is, the most common) type of participant. In this study, that would be a black non-Hispanic woman who lives in Brooklyn, has one child, has 12 or more years of education, is between the ages of 20 and 30, and is not a long-term welfare recipient. These figures, when multiplied by 100, represent the percentage-point change in probability of achieving a given outcome resulting from a one-unit change in the independent variable. A marginal effect of 0.015, for example, would represent a 1.5 percentage-point increase in the probably of the outcome, such as job placement. To assist readers in gauging how important various percentage-point changes are, Table C.1 shows the outcomes for the modal and average participant for comparison.

Tables C.2 through C.6 present the regression results. Note that Tables C.3, C.4, and C.5 show results for placed custodial participants only, meaning those who become employed. Table C.6 defines performance using the study's best measure of sustained employment—the probability of being placed in a job and still working at any job six months later among all participants. This measure gets closest to the main question of this study: Which factors affect programs' abilities to help people become and stay employed?

Table C.1 Participant Outcomes (%)

	Performance measure			
	Job placement	Job placement with a high wage (among placed participants)	Placed in job and still working at any job six months later (among placed participants)	Placed in job and still working at any job six months later (among all participants)
Custodial participants				
Modal	22.0	21.6	37.8	8.3
Average	16.6	18.4	46.1	7.7
Noncustodial participants				
Modal	21.8	21.1	38.5	8.4
Average	19.2	16.8	43.3	8.3
All participants				
Modal	21.8	21.6	37.8	8.2
Average	17.7	17.6	44.8	7.9

NOTE: Average outcomes are provided for comparison, although regression results present marginal effects for the modal individual. Averages may differ slightly from those reported in the text because this table presents averages among individuals ($N = 14,079$) while averages in the text are at the program level ($N = 26$).

Table C.2 The Effects of Participant Characteristics, Economic Environment, and Organizational Characteristics on Performance, Measured as Job Placement for Custodial Participants

Characteristic	Marginal effect	Z-value	Standard error
Participant characteristics			
12+ years of education	0.059***	0.000	0.011
Long-term welfare recipient (5+ years lifetime)	−0.076***	0.000	0.011
Male	0.018	0.327	0.018
<20 years old	−0.054*	0.087	0.032
20–29 years old	−0.025	0.107	0.016
30–39 years old	0.006	0.699	0.016
40 or older (omitted category)			
1 custodial child	0.0002	0.990	0.015
2 custodial children	0.008	0.618	0.016
3+ custodial children (omitted category)			
Black, non-Hispanic	0.001	0.983	0.030
Hispanic	0.029	0.368	0.033
Asian	−0.117**	0.035	0.055
Other	0.065	0.159	0.046
White, non-Hispanic (omitted category)			
Economic environment			
ESP in Brooklyn	0.015	0.376	0.017
ESP in Bronx	0.001	0.949	0.018
ESP in Queens	0.029	0.218	0.024
ESP in Staten Island	0.056	0.167	0.040
ESP in Manhattan (omitted category)			
Program characteristics			
For-profit	0.002	0.914	0.015
EarnFair Alliance member	−0.049***	0.004	0.017
Deassignment rate	−0.001	0.656	0.001
Training referrals	−0.008***	0.000	0.002
Length of time to median placement (among placed)	0.009[a]**	0.039	0.004
Length of time to median placement (among placed) squared	−0.0001[a]**	0.022	0.00003

(continued)

Table C.2 (continued)

NOTE: *** significant at the 0.01 level; ** significant at the 0.05 level; and * significant at the 0.10 level. The model is based on a logit transformation of the expected probability, and the distribution of the error term is logistic. Individuals are clustered by sites. The values are marginal effects for the modal custodial participant and, when multiplied by 100, represent the percentage-point change in the probability of achieving the outcome. The dependent variable is dichotomous, indicating whether a participant was placed in a job or not. The sample size is 26 at the site level and 8,103 at the individual level.

[a] Length of time to median placement and its square are jointly significant at the 0.01 level.

Table C.3 The Effects of Participant Characteristics, Economic Environment, and Organizational Characteristics on Performance, Measured as Job Placement with a High Wage for Placed Custodial Participants

Characteristic	Marginal effect	Z-value	Standard error
Participant characteristics			
12+ years of education	0.091***	0.000	0.024
Long-term welfare recipient (5+ years lifetime)	−0.105***	0.000	0.025
Male	0.005	0.887	0.035
<20 years old	−0.126**	0.012	0.050
20–29 years old	−0.099**	0.012	0.039
30–39 years old	0.040	0.247	0.035
40 or older (omitted category)			
1 custodial child	0.076***	0.005	0.027
2 custodial children	0.031	0.423	0.039
3+ custodial children (omitted category)			
Black, non-Hispanic	−0.057	0.374	0.064
Hispanic	−0.052	0.223	0.043
Asian	−0.039	0.800	0.155
Other	−0.092	0.115	0.058
White, non-Hispanic (omitted category)			
Economic environment			
ESP in Brooklyn	0.015	0.710	0.041
ESP in Bronx	0.042	0.374	0.047
ESP in Queens	0.061	0.307	0.060
ESP in Staten Island	−0.047	0.450	0.062
ESP in Manhattan (omitted category)			
Program characteristics			
For-profit	0.047	0.218	0.038
EarnFair Alliance member	0.145***	0.006	0.052
Deassignment rate	−0.001	0.704	0.002
Training referrals	0.005	0.115	0.003
Length of time to median placement (among placed participants)	0.002*	0.081	0.001

NOTE: *** significant at the 0.01 level; ** significant at the 0.05 level; and * significant at the 0.10 level. The model is based on a logit transformation of the expected probability, and the distribution of the error term is logistic. Individuals are clustered by sites. The values are marginal effects for the modal custodial participant and, when multiplied by 100, represent the percentage-point change in the probability of achieving the outcome. The dependent variable is dichotomous, indicating whether a placed participant received a "high wage" or not. High wage is defined by the HRA as paying at least $344 per week. The sample size is 26 at the site level and 1,345 at the individual level.

Table C.4 The Effects of Participant Characteristics, Economic Environment, and Organizational Characteristics on Performance, Measured as Three-Month Employment Retention for Placed Custodial Participants

Characteristic	Marginal effect	Z-value	Standard error
Participant characteristics			
12+ years of education	0.038	0.180	0.028
Long-term welfare recipient (5+ years lifetime)	−0.066*	0.034	0.031
Male	−0.040	0.352	0.043
<20 years old	−0.109	0.274	0.099
20–29 years old	−0.116***	0.000	0.032
30–39 years old	−0.009	0.815	0.038
40 or older (omitted category)			
1 custodial child	0.083**	0.026	0.037
2 custodial children	0.032	0.347	0.034
3+ custodial children (omitted category)			
Black, non-Hispanic	0.065	0.373	0.073
Hispanic	0.074	0.230	0.062
Asian	0.209	0.135	0.140
Other	0.027	0.756	0.088
White, non-Hispanic (omitted category)			
Economic environment			
ESP in Brooklyn	0.036	0.400	0.043
ESP in Bronx	0.038	0.345	0.040
ESP in Queens	−0.049	0.363	0.054
ESP in Staten Island	0.006	0.941	0.080
ESP in Manhattan (omitted category)			
Program characteristics			
For-profit	0.033	0.328	0.034
EarnFair Alliance member	−0.041	0.367	0.045
Deassignment rate	0.001	0.598	0.002
Training referrals	0.003	0.493	0.004
Length of time to median placement (among placed participants)	−0.0004	0.757	0.001

NOTE: *** significant at the 0.01 level; ** significant at the 0.05 level; and * significant at the 0.10 level. The model is based on a logit transformation of the expected probability, and the distribution of the error term is logistic. Individuals are clustered by sites. The values are marginal effects for the modal custodial participant and, when multiplied by 100, represent the percentage-point change in the probability of achieving the outcome. The dependent variable is dichotomous, indicating whether a placed participant was still working three months later at any job or not. The sample size is 26 at the site level and 1,345 at the individual level.

Table C.5 The Effects of Participant Characteristics, Economic Environment, and Organizational Characteristics on Performance, Measured as Six-Month Employment Retention for Placed Custodial Participants

Characteristic	Marginal effect	Z-value	Standard error
Participant characteristics			
12+ years of education	0.093***	0.001	0.029
Long-term welfare recipient (5+ years lifetime)	−0.068**	0.029	0.031
Male	−0.052	0.236	0.044
<20 years old	−0.100	0.310	0.098
20–29 years old	−0.081**	0.028	0.037
30–39 years old	0.022	0.553	0.038
40 or older (omitted category)			
1 custodial child	0.022	0.561	0.038
2 custodial children	0.005	0.905	0.039
3+ custodial children (omitted category)			
Black, non-Hispanic	−0.004	0.959	0.073
Hispanic	0.023	0.757	0.075
Asian	−0.068	0.780	0.244
Other	0.028	0.763	0.094
White, non-Hispanic (omitted category)			
Economic environment			
ESP in Brooklyn	0.090	0.108	0.056
ESP in Bronx	0.032	0.581	0.057
ESP in Queens	0.015	0.832	0.070
ESP in Staten Island	−0.073	0.500	0.108
ESP in Manhattan (omitted category)			
Program characteristics			
For-profit	−0.002	0.967	0.049
EarnFair Alliance member	0.007	0.907	0.056
Deassignment rate	0.001	0.821	0.003
Training referrals	−0.007	0.213	0.005
Length of time to median placement (among placed participants)	0.00002	0.992	0.002

NOTE: *** significant at the 0.01 level; ** significant at the 0.05 level; and * significant at the 0.10 level. The model is based on a logit transformation of the expected probability, and the distribution of the error term is logistic. Individuals are clustered by sites. The values are marginal effects for the modal custodial participant and, when multiplied by 100, represent the percentage-point change in the probability of achieving the outcome. The dependent variable is dichotomous, indicating whether a placed participant was still working six months later at any job or not. The sample size is 26 at the site level and 1,345 at the individual level.

Table C.6 The Effects of Participant Characteristics, Economic Environment, and Organizational Characteristics on Performance, Measured as Placed in a Job and Still Working at Any Job Six Months Later for Custodial Participants

Characteristic	Marginal effect	Z-value	Standard error
Participant characteristics			
12+ years of education	0.047***	0.000	0.009
Long-term welfare recipient (5+ years lifetime)	−0.049***	0.000	0.009
Male	−0.005	0.731	0.014
<20 years old	−0.042*	0.071	0.023
20–29 years old	−0.037**	0.012	0.015
30–39 years old	0.008	0.537	0.013
40 or older (omitted category)			
1 custodial child	0.004	0.737	0.012
2 custodial children	0.004	0.765	0.013
3+ custodial children (omitted category)			
Black, non-Hispanic	−0.003	0.914	0.024
Hispanic	0.017	0.522	0.027
Asian	−0.070*	0.059	0.037
Other	0.046	0.249	0.040
White, non-Hispanic (omitted category)			
Economic environment			
ESP in Brooklyn	0.028*	0.092	0.017
ESP in Bronx	0.016	0.488	0.022
ESP in Queens	0.026	0.373	0.029
ESP in Staten Island	0.012	0.784	0.042
ESP in Manhattan (omitted category)			
Program characteristics			
For-profit	0.003	0.861	0.017
EarnFair Alliance member	−0.022	0.211	0.017
Deassignment rate	−0.001	0.155	0.001
Training referrals	−0.005**	0.015	0.002
Length of time to median placement (among placed participants)	−0.0002	0.681	0.0005

NOTE: *** significant at the 0.01 level; ** significant at the 0.05 level; and * significant at the 0.10 level. The model is based on a logit transformation of the expected probability, and the distribution of the error term is logistic. Individuals are clustered by sites. The values are marginal effects for the modal custodial participant and, when multiplied by 100, represent the percentage-point change in the probability of achieving the outcome. The dependent variable is dichotomous, indicating whether a participant was placed in a job and was still working at any job six months later or not. The sample size is 26 at the site level and 8,103 at the individual level.

References

Acs, Gregory, and Pamela Loprest. 2004. *Leaving Welfare: Employment and Well-Being of Families that Left Welfare in the Post-Entitlement Era.* Kalamazoo, MI: W.E. Upjohn Institute for Employment Research.

Bardach, Eugene. 1993. *Improving the Productivity of JOBS Programs.* New York: MDRC.

Behn, Robert D. 1991. *Leadership Counts: Lessons for Public Managers from the Massachusetts Welfare, Training, and Employment Program.* Cambridge, MA: Harvard University Press.

Berg, Linnea, Lynn Olson, and Aimee Conrad. 1991. "Causes and Implications of Rapid Job Loss among Participants in a Welfare-to-Work Program." Paper presented at the Annual Research Conference of the Association for Public Policy and Management, held in Bethesda, MD, October 24–26.

Besharov, Douglas J., and Peter Germanis. 2004. "Full-Engagement Welfare in New York City: Lessons for TANF's Participation Requirements." Washington, DC: American Enterprise Institute.

Bloom, Dan, and Charles Michalopoulos. 2001. *How Welfare and Work Policies Affect Employment and Income: A Synthesis of Research.* New York: MDRC.

Bloom, Dan, and Don Winstead. 2002. "Sanctions and Welfare Reform." Policy Brief No. 12. Washington, DC: Brookings Institution.

Bloom, Howard S., Carolyn J. Hill, and James A. Riccio. 2003. "Linking Program Implementation and Effectiveness: Lessons from a Pooled Sample of Welfare-to-Work Experiments." *Journal of Policy Analysis and Management* 22(4): 551–575.

Bouchikhi, Hamid, and John R. Kimberly. 2003. "Escaping the Identity Trap." *Sloan Management Review* 44(3): 20–26.

Brown, Trevor, and Matt Potoski. 2006. "Contracting for Management: Assessing Management Capacity under Alternative Service Delivery Arrangements." *Journal of Policy Analysis and Management* 25(2): 323–346.

Burtless, Gary. 2004. "The Labor Force Status of Mothers Who Are Most Likely to Receive Welfare: Changes Following Reform." Brookings Web Editorial. Washington, DC: Brookings Institution. http://www.brookings.edu/opinions/2004/0330childrenfamilies_burtless.aspx (accessed May 12, 2010).

Clark, James. 2005. "Overcoming Opposition and Giving Work Experience to Welfare Applicants and Recipients." In *Managing Welfare Reform in New York City*, E. S. Savas, ed. Oxford: Rowman & Littlefield, pp. 171–222.

Council of Economic Advisers. 1999. "The Effects of Welfare Policy and the Economic Expansion on Welfare Caseloads: An Update." Washington, DC:

Council of Economic Advisers. http://clinton4.nara.gov/WH/EOP/CEA/html/welfare/ (accessed May 12, 2010).

Dawson, K., and Berry, M. 2002. "Engaging Families in Child Welfare Services: An Evidence-Based Approach to Best Practice." *Child Welfare* 81(2): 293–317.

Dees, J. Gregory, and Beth Battle Anderson. 2004. "Sector-Bending: Blurring the Lines between Nonprofit and For-Profit." In *In Search of the Nonprofit Sector*, Peter Frumkin and Jonathan B. Imber, eds. New Brunswick, NJ: Transaction Publishers, pp. 51–71.

Dunifon, Rachel, and Greg J. Duncan. 1998. "Long-Run Effects of Motivation on Labor-Market Success." *Social Psychology Quarterly* 61(1): 33–48.

Eggleston, Karen, Nolan Miller, and Richard Zeckhauser. 2001. "A Dynamic Model of Nonprofit Behavior." Kennedy School working paper. Cambridge, MA: Harvard University.

Frumkin, Peter, and Alice Andre-Clark. 2000. "When Missions, Markets, and Politics Collide: Values and Strategy in the Nonprofit Human Services." *Nonprofit and Voluntary Sector Quarterly* 29(Suppl. 1): 141–163.

Greenberg, David, Victoria Deitch, and Gayle Hamilton. 2009. "Welfare-to-Work Program Benefits and Costs." New York: MDRC.

Grønbjerg, Kirsten A. 2001. "The U.S. Nonprofit Human Service Sector: A Creeping Revolution." *Nonprofit and Voluntary Sector Quarterly* 30(2): 276–297.

Hamilton, Gayle. 2002. "Moving People from Welfare to Work: Lessons from the National Evaluation of Welfare-to-Work Strategies." New York: MDRC.

Heinrich, Carolyn J. 2000. "Organizational Form and Performance: An Empirical Investigation of Nonprofit and For-Profit Job-Training Service Providers." *Journal of Policy Analysis and Management* 19(2): 233–261.

Hershey, Alan, and LaDonna Pavetti. 1997. "Turning Job-Finders into Job-Keepers." *Future of Children* 7(1): 74–86.

Hollister, Robinson G. 2008. "Hollister Response to Richard Nathan's Opening Statement." *Journal of Policy Analysis and Management* 27(3): 611–615.

Hollister, Robinson G., Peter Kemper, and Rebecca A. Maynard. 1984. *The National Supported Work Demonstration*. Madison, WI: University of Wisconsin Press.

Holzer, Harry J., and Douglas A. Wissoker. 2001. *How Can We Encourage Job Retention and Advancement for Welfare Recipients?* Washington, DC: Urban Institute Press.

Kettl, Donald F. 2006. "Government Performance: Why Management Matters; Government Matters: Welfare Reform in Wisconsin; How Management Matters: Street-Level Bureaucrats and Welfare Reform." *Journal of Policy Analysis and Management* 25(2): 503–510.

Lewis, Robert E. 1991. "What Elements of Service Relate to Treatment Goal Achievement?" In *Families in Crisis: The Impact of Intensive Family Preservation Services*, M. W. Fraser, P. J. Pecora, and D. A. Haapala, eds. Hawthorne, NY: Aldine de Gruyter, pp. 225–272.

March, James G. 1994. *A Primer on Decision Making*. New York: Free Press.

Mead, Lawrence M. 1983. "Expectations and Welfare Work: WIN in New York City." *Policy Studies Review* 2(4): 648–662.

———. 1997. "Optimizing JOBS: Evaluation versus Administration." *Public Administration Review* 57(2): 113–123.

———. 2003. "Performance Analysis." In *Policy into Action: Implementation Research and Welfare Reform*, Mary Clair Lennon and Thomas Corbett, eds. Washington, DC: Urban Institute Press, pp. 107–144.

Meyers, Marcia K., Bonnie Glaser, and Karin MacDonald. 1998. "On the Front Lines of Welfare Delivery: Are Workers Implementing Policy Reforms?" *Journal of Policy Analysis and Management* 17(1): 1–22.

Mitchell, John J., Mark L. Chadwin, and Demetra S. Nightingale. 1980. *Implementing Welfare-Employment Programs: An Institutional Analysis of the Work Incentive (WIN) Program*. Washington DC: U.S. Department of Labor.

Moore, Mark H. 2000. "Managing for Value: Organizational Strategy in For-Profit, Nonprofit, and Governmental Organizations." *Nonprofit and Voluntary Sector Quarterly* 29(Supplement 1): 183–208.

Needleman, Jack. 2001. "The Role of Nonprofits in Health Care." *Journal of Health Politics, Policy and Law* 26(5): 1113–1130.

New York City Human Resources Administration. 2009a. Cash Assistance Reports. New York: City of New York. http:www.nyc.gov/html/hra/html/statistics/cash_assistance_reports.shtml (accessed September 1, 2010).

———. 2009b. Facts. New York: City of New York. http://www.nyc.gov/html/hra/html/statistics/hra_facts.shtml (accessed September 1, 2010).

Nightingale, Demetra S. 2005. "Overview of Welfare Reform." In *Managing Welfare Reform in New York City*, E. S. Savas, ed. Oxford: Rowman & Littlefield, pp. 18–56.

Olson, Lynn, Linnea Berg, and Aimee Conrad. 1990. "High Job Turnover among the Urban Poor: The Project Match Experience." Unpublished paper. Chicago: Center for Urban Affairs and Policy Research.

O'Neill, June, and Sanders Korenman. 2005. "The Welfare Revolution in New York City." In *Managing Welfare Reform in New York City*, E. S. Savas, ed. Oxford: Rowman & Littlefield, pp. 301–351.

Peck, Laura R., and Ronald J. Scott Jr. 2005. "Can Welfare Case Management Increase Employment? Evidence from a Pilot Program Evaluation." *Policy Studies Journal* 33(4): 509–533.

Raudenbush, Stephen W., and Anthony S. Bryk. 2002. *Hierarchical Linear*

Models: Applications and Data Analysis Methods. Thousand Oaks, CA: SAGE Publications.

Riccio, James A., and Alan Orenstein. 1996. "Understanding Best Practices for Operating Welfare-to-Work Programs." *Evaluation Review* 20(1): 3–28.

Riccucci, Norma M. 2005. *How Management Matters: Street-Level Bureaucrats and Welfare Reform.* Washington, DC: Georgetown University Press.

Salamon, Lester M. 1993. "The Marketization of Welfare: Changing Nonprofit and For-Profit Roles in the American Welfare State." *Social Service Review* 67(1): 16–39.

Sandfort, Jodi R. 2000. "Examining the Effect of Welfare-to-Work Structures and Services on a Desired Policy Outcome." In *Governance and Performance: New Perspectives*, Carolyn Heinrich and Laurence Lynn, eds. Washington, DC: Georgetown University Press, pp. 140–165.

Sanger, M. Bryna. 2003. *The Welfare Marketplace: Privatization and Welfare Reform.* Washington, DC: Brookings Institution Press.

Schwartz, Joel. 2004. "Work and Poverty." *The Public Interest* 157(Fall): 131–135. http://www.nationalaffairs.com/doclib/20080710_200415710workandpovertyjoelschwartz.pdf (accessed May 12, 2010).

Scrivener, Susan, Gilda Azurdia, and Jocelyn Page. 2005. "The Employment Retention and Advancement Project: Results from the South Carolina ERA Site." New York: MDRC.

Seefeldt, Kristin S. 2008. *Working after Welfare: How Women Balance Jobs and Family in the Wake of Welfare Reform.* Kalamazoo, MI: W.E. Upjohn Institute for Employment Research.

Sherwood, Kay E. 2005. "Managing the Welfare System with JobStat." In *Managing Welfare Reform in New York City*, E. S. Savas, ed. Oxford: Rowman & Littlefield, pp. 105–146.

Strawn, Julie, and Karin Martinson. 2000. *Steady Work and Better Jobs: How to Help Low-Income Parents Sustain Employment and Advance in the Workforce.* New York: MDRC.

U.S. Department of Health and Human Services. 2006. *Characteristics and Financial Circumstances of TANF Recipients, Fiscal Year 2004.* Washington, DC: HHS, Administration for Children and Families. http://www.acf.hhs.gov/programs/ofa/character/FY2004/indexfy04.htm (accessed September 1, 2010).

———. 2009. *Caseload Data 2009.* Washington, DC: HHS, Administration for Children and Families. http:www.acf.hhs.gov/programs/ofa/data-reports/caseload/caseload_current.htm#2009 (accessed September 1, 2010).

Wagner, Suzanne L., Toby Herr, Charles Change, and Diana Brooks. 1998. *Five Years of Welfare: Too Long? Too Short? Lessons from Project Match's Longitudinal Tracking Data.* Chicago: Project Match, Erikson Institute.

Walker, Robert, David Greenberg, Karl Ashworth, and Andreas Cebulla. 2003. "Successful Welfare-to-Work Programs: Were Riverside and Portland Really That Good?" *Focus* 22(3): 11–18.

Wavelet, Melissa, and Jacquie Anderson. 2002. "Promoting Self-Sufficiency: What We Know about Sustaining Employment and Increasing Income among Welfare Recipients and the Working Poor." *Focus* 22(1): 56–62.

Weisbroad, Burton A. 1998. "Modeling the Nonprofit Organization as a Multiproduct Firm: A Framework for Choice." In *To Profit or Not to Profit: The Commercial Transformation of the Nonprofit Sector*, Burton A. Weisbroad, ed. New York: Cambridge University Press, pp. 47–64.

Weiss, Robert S. 1994. *Learning From Strangers: The Art and Method of Qualitative Interview Studies*. New York: Free Press.

Youdelman, Sondra. 2005. "The Revolving Door: Research Findings on NYC's Employment Services and Placement System and Its Effectiveness in Moving People from Welfare to Work." New York: Community Voices Heard. http://cvh.mayfirst.org/files/The Revolving Door - Full Report.pdf (accessed May 12, 2010).

The Author

Andrew R. Feldman is executive assistant at the Wisconsin Department of Workforce Development, one of the top three leaders at the agency. His previous positions include senior policy advisor to Wisconsin Governor Jim Doyle, instructor in public management at Harvard's Kennedy School of Government, special assistant to the secretary of administration and finance in Massachusetts, staff economist on President Clinton's Council of Economic Advisers, and special assistant to the president at MDRC in New York City. A native of Milwaukee, Feldman earned his BA in economics from Swarthmore College and an MA and a PhD in Public Policy from Harvard University.

Index

The italic letters *f, n,* and *t* following a page number indicate that the subject information of the heading is within a figure, note, or table, respectively, on that page. Double italics indicate multiple but consecutive elements.

Affiliated Computer Services (ACS, firm), 20, 28*n*3, 90
Aid to Families with Dependent Children (AFDC). *See its successor*, Temporary Assistance to Needy Families (TANF) program
America Works (firm)
  ESP program of, 20, 21*t*
  management of, 62, 71, 72, 81, 90
American Recovery and Reinvestment Act (2009), TANF and, 6, 16*n*5
Anger, overcoming, 34–35
Apprehension, overcoming, 13, 14, 43, 45, 47, 72
Apprenticeships, 3, 4
Asian persons, 150t
  regression results on, 159*t*, 161*t*, 162*t*, 163*t*, 164*t*

Behavioral expectations
  ESP programs and, 24, 35–36, 46
  spirit of partnership and, 8, 33–34, 34, 38–39, 41–42*n*2
  workplace norms in, 73, 113–114
Black non-Hispanic persons
  as NYC vs. U.S. TANF participants, 150*t*, 157
  regression results on, 159*t*, 161*t*, 162*t*, 163*t*, 164*t*
Bonuses, performance incentives as, 20, 20*f*, 74, 108–109
Borough of Manhattan Community College, ESP program of, 21*t*
Bronx, NYC
  ESP programs in, 21t, 159*t*, 161*t*, 162*t*, 163*t*, 164*t*
  welfare recipients in, 150–151

Brooklyn, NYC
  ESP program in, 159*t*, 161*t*, 162*t*, 163*t*, 164*t*
  welfare recipients in, 150–151
  welfare-to-work programs in, 2, 21*t*

California
  safety-net policy in, 22–23
  welfare-to-work programs in, 1, 11–12, 41–42*n*2, 130
Career advancement
  staff who promote, 39–40, 47–48, 95–96
  tension between, and motherhood, 5
Career and Education Consultants (firm), 21*t*, 52, 79, 91
Career counseling, 4, 79, 144
  reemployment services and, 64–65
  See also Case-management approach to welfare reform
Case-management approach to welfare reform, 62
  case managers in, 14–15, 17*n*15, 65, 72, 73
  ESP participants and, 23–24, 29*n*7, 48–49, 54, 58–59*n*3
  job readiness and, 13–15, 17*n*15, 43, 75
  quick-placement vs., 13–15, 16*n*11, 16*n*13, 59*n*7, 69–77, 76*f*, 111–112, 117*nn*12–13, 142, 151*n*2
  rationale for, 75–77
  retention outcomes and, 64–66, 66*nn*2–3
Caseloads. *See* Welfare caseloads
Cash assistance, 1, 3
Catholic Charities, Bronx, ESP program of, 21*t*

173

CBOs. *See* Community-based organizations
Center for Employment Training, San Jose, behavioral workplace norms and, 41–42*n*2
Center for Family Life, Brooklyn, ESP program of, 21*t*
Certificate training, 24, 36
Child care
  custodial persons and, 14, 71, 88*n*2
  overcoming, as employment barrier, 13, 19, 45, 73
Child support, enforcement of, xv
Children, number of custodial, 150*t*
Citizens Action Bureau, Brooklyn, ESP program of, 21*t*
Communication, 94, 96, 130
  effective informal and religious, 99–100
  evidence-based, and program improvements, 142–144
  imperfect information as suboptimal practice in, 139–140
Community-based organizations (CBOs), 113
  EarnFair Alliance among, 92–95, 94*f*
  employment programs and compensation of, 92–93, 101*n*6
Community colleges, 8, 21*t*, 142
Community development organizations, 99
  SEEDCO among, 92–96, 101*n*6
Competition, 101*n*, 113
  as motivation among staff, 74, 87*n*4
CompStat, adaptation of, 21
Confrontational attitudes, overcoming, 37, 45–46
Cove, Peter, quoted on management issues, 62, 71, 72, 81, 90
Creaming opportunities
  deassignments and sanctions, 125, 126*n*2, 127*f*
  employee retention and, 40, 42*n*4, 91
  employment services, 126, 126*n*3, 127*f*
  program entry, 124–125

Curan, Charlotte, quoted on management issues, 90
Custodial vs. noncustodial persons, 150*t*
  effective practices with, 105–106
  employee retention of, 10–11, 106, 117*nn*9–10
  job placement and, 13, 109, 110–111, 116*n*4, 117*n*7
  welfare benefits eligibility of, 23, 29*n*6
Cypress Hills Local Development Corp., Brooklyn, ESP program of, 21*t*

Deassignment, 112
  creaming opportunities for, 125, 126*n*2, 127*f*
  ESP programs and, 82–84, 83*f*, 91, 92*f*, 100, 100*f*, 101*nn*2–3, 102*n*11, 149*t*, 159*t*, 161*t*, 162*t*, 163*t*, 164*t*
  program size and, 97, 97*f*
  SEEDCO and, from EarnFair programs, 94*f*, 101–102*n*7
Dependence, reducing, 5, 48, 49, 76*f*, 120, 133
Disabled adults, employment and training assistance for, 4, 14, 44, 82
Domestic abuse, as significant employment barrier, 14

Earned Income Tax Credit, 24
  welfare caseload reduction and, xv, 5, 16*n*6
EarnFair Alliance
  deassignment from, 101–102*n*7
  founding and operations of, 92–95, 94*f*
  membership in, 159*t*, 161*t*, 162*t*, 163*t*, 164*t*
  performance incentives and, 108–109, 140–141
Earnings, 6, 114
East New York Development Corp., Brooklyn, ESP program of, 21*t*

Economic conditions
  legislation to stimulate (*see* American Recovery and Reinvestment Act [2009])
  strengthening, 28
  strong, 5, 16n6
  weak, 3, 6, 28, 29n13
Education, 5
  NYC study participants, level, 150t, 159t, 161t, 162t, 163t, 164t
Education and training programs, 4
  NYC use of, different from typical past, 11–12, 16n10
Education-first welfare reform, xviii, 3
  quality of, 12, 16n12
Employers
  associations of, as short-term job training providers, 8, 24–25, 79
  relationships with, as source of job placements, 52, 54–55
Employment and training assistance, TAA and, 4
Employment barriers, 13–14, 44–46, 50n2
  manageable vs. significant, 14
  serious, and deassignment from ESP programs, 82–84, 101–102n7
  staff who address, 46–47, 49
  time needed to address, 75–76, 76f
Employment counselors. *See* Career counseling; Case-management approach to welfare reform
Employment programs, 3, 29n6, 115
  administrative organizations for (*see* Faith-based vs. secular organizations as employment service providers; Government vs. private organizations as employment service providers; Nonprofit vs. profit organizations as ESP providers)
  size of, in NYC, 95–98, 97f, 102nn8–10
  specialized, for people with significant barriers, 14, 24, 28n1, 82

  See also Service providers
Employment rates
  boost in, 5, 116
  caseload, by NYC site, 132–134, 133f, 138f
  ESP programs and, 26–27, 26f, 29n12, 105
  nonprofit vs. profit programs and, 121–123, 122f, 126, 127f
Employment retention
  "creaming" and, 40, 42n4, 91, 124–126
  custodial vs. noncustodial persons and, 10–11, 106
  job training and, 79, 110, 117nn8–9
  pay-for-performance dollars with bonuses for, 20, 20f, 25, 58, 64, 66n1
  placement rates vs., 57–58, 57f, 58n2, 59n4, 77, 105, 106–108, 107f, 108f, 126, 127f
  techniques in, 62–64, 123
  work-first providers and promotion of, 8f, 9, 27, 27f, 52, 61–66, 116, 143–144
Employment Service and Placement (ESP) programs, 14, 23–28, 28n2
  activities of, 23–25, 29nn7–9, 62–64
  business orientation of, 59nn6–7, 89–91, 99, 120
  deassignment from, 82–84, 83f, 91, 92f, 100, 100f, 101nn2–3
  dropouts and sanction rates, 86–87, 88n11, 91–92, 100f, 116
  nonprofit vs. profit organizations with, in NYC, 7, 19–20, 21t, 74, 89–92, 92f, 96f, 101n5, 101nn2–3, 106–108, 107f, 119–126, 127ff
  program performance of, 25–28, 26f, 27f, 29nn10–13, 57–58
  staff compensation in (*see* Performance-based contracts)
Engagement approach, creating partnership with, 40
English limitations, as significant employment barrier, 14, 82

ESP programs. *See* Employment Service and Placement programs
Ex-felons, 29*n*6, 47–48

Facilitators as program staff, 43, 46, 54
Faith-based vs. secular organizations as employment service providers, 90, 96*f*, 98–101, 100*f*, 114
Family problems, overcoming, 13, 46
Family sanctions, full vs. partial, 22
FEGS (organization), Brooklyn, ESP program of, 21*t*
Feldman, Andrew R., xv, 171
Forrester, William, quoted on management issues, 89
Frontline management
  literature overview, 129–130
  practices of, and program performance, 15, 129
  service strategies vs., and effectiveness, 134–138, 138*f*

GAIN (Greater Avenues for Independence), 11–12, 16*n*11, 130
Gaming the system, 66, 86, 99, 153
Giuliani, Mayor Rudolph, workfare program of, 22
Goodwill Industries, 20, 21*t*, 74, 89
Government vs. private organizations as employment service providers, 1, 19, 98
Greater Avenues for Independence (GAIN), 11–12, 16*n*11, 130
Guided job search, 153–156
  arguments against, 155
  effectiveness of job developers vs., 155–156
  as primary tool, 154, 156*f*
  rationale for, 153–154

Harlem Congregations for Community Improvement, Manhattan, ESP program of, 21*t*
Henry Street Settlement, Manhattan, ESP program of, 21*t*
Hispanic persons, 150*t*
  regression results on, 159*t*, 161*t*, 162*t*, 163*t*, 164*t*
Homelessness, as significant employment barrier, 14, 44, 84
Houston, Texas, private providers of welfare-to-work services in, 1
HRA. *See* New York City (NYC), Human Resources Administration
Human-capital-development programs. *See* Skill-building programs
Human resources personnel, job developers as, 55

Illinois, postprogram employee retention in, 61–62
Illiteracy, as significant employment barrier, 14, 82, 83
Independent job search, 58*n*1, 153, 156*n*1
Interviews, 45, 71
  preparing ESP participants for, 43, 54, 72, 73–74

Job applications, not knowing how to fill out, 45
Job developers, 37
  case managers and, 14–15, 17*n*15, 65
  as intermediaries in job matching, 8–9, 24, 38, 51–52, 64
  payment of, 58, 59*nn*6–7, 74
  placement rates and, 56, 58*n*2, 87*n*9
  quick-placement sites and, 72–73
  techniques used by, 53–55
Job matching, 117*n*8
  good, by work-first providers, 8–9, 8*f*, 51–59
  upgrading and, 64, 77
Job Opportunities and Basic Skills (JOBS), 12
Job placement, 13, 52, 53
  case managers and, 14, 73, 77
  ESP active participants and, 27, 27*f*, 29*n*13, 56, 87*n*9, 105, 106–108, 107*f*, 108*f*
  nonprofit vs. profit programs and, 121–123, 122*f*

Job placement, *cont.*
  pay-for-performance dollars for, 20, 20*f*, 72
  time taken to start, 69–71, 70*f*, 72, 73, 87*n*1, 92, 92*f*, 94*f*, 95, 97*f*, 98, 99, 100–101, 100*f*, 101*n*5, 137–138, 138*f*, 149*t*, 151*nn*3–4, 159*t*, 161*t*, 162*t*, 163*t*, 164*t*
Job readiness
  case management and, 13–15, 69, 75–76
  ESP programs and, workshops, 38, 73–74
  various approaches to, 49
  work-first providers and development of, 8, 8*f*, 9, 19, 24, 43–50
Job search assistance, 4, 19, 117*n*7
  employability assessment in, 71–72, 110
  types of, 53, 58*n*1, 80, 109, 153–156
Job skills, 5
  specific, in NYC training, 11, 16*n*10, 79, 87*n*6
Job-training programs, 3
  common approaches to, 80–81
  dropouts from, 81, 82, 117*n*6
  ESPs in NYC with, 70*f*, 110, 137–138, 138*f*, 149*t*
  on-the-job training among, 4, 12, 87*n*5
  rationale for, 79, 87*n*6, 97–98, 111
  rationale for discouraging, 81–82, 87*n*8, 94–95, 100, 109–111, 115–116, 117*n*11
  short-term, and work-first providers, 8, 12, 24–25, 72, 77–79
  voucher rules for, 16*n*10, 29*n*8, 78, 80, 87*n*7, 101*n*4
Joblessness. *See* Unemployment
JOBS (Job Opportunities and Basic Skills), 12
JobStat, HRA and, 21–22, 28–29*n*5, 28*n*4

Labor-force-attachment programs. *See* Work-first welfare reform
Laguardia Community College, ESP program of, 21*t*
Leadership vs. management, 129–138
  program performance and, 15, 143–144, 144*n*1
Lockheed Martin (firm), welfare-to-work services of, 28*n*3
Low-income workers, 4
  custodial vs. noncustodial, 23, 29*n*6, 106, 150*t*
  low skills of, 5, 46
  supports for, 5, 16*n*6, 79, 105, 144
  workplace norms and, 42*n*2, 113–114

Managerial incompetence, 142–143
Manhattan, NYC, 21*t*, 150–151
MDRC (firm), xviii–xix
Medicaid, fear of losing, 45, 50*n*3
Melocarro, Susan, quoted on management issues, 52, 79, 91
Men
  characteristics of, as NYC study participants, 150*t*
  employee retention of, as noncustodial persons, 10, 106, 111–112, 117*n*14
  welfare benefits eligibility of, as noncustodial persons, 23, 29*n*6, 114–115, 117*n*15
Mental disabilities, 4
  as significant employment barrier, 14, 44, 82
Michigan, independent job search used in, 156*n*1
Milwaukee, Wisconsin, private welfare-to-work services in, 1, 19
Minimum wage, 5, 16*n*6, 77
Mothers
  employment rates of, 5
  never-married, 5, 23, 27–28, 46
Motivation
  competition among staff and, 74, 87*n*4
  deassignment of those without, 82–84, 83*f*, 91
  lack of, as employment barrier, 44, 50*n*2, 66*n*2

Motivation, cont.
staff who address lack of, 47–49, 71
staff who lack, themselves, 81–82

New York City College of Technology, ESP program of, 21t
New York City (NYC), Human Resources Administration (HRA)
accountability tools used by, 21–22, 28n4, 28–29n5
high wage as defined by, 57, 59n5, 106
Job Centers run by, 17n15, 19, 24, 34, 82, 91
provider contracts with, 93–94, 101n6
sanctions and, 22, 25–26, 29n11, 34, 143
TANF caseloads and, 15–16n2
training vouchers from, 16n10, 24–25, 29n8, 78, 94f
New York City (NYC) boroughs. See specifics, e.g., Brooklyn, NYC; Staten Island, NYC
New York City (NYC) welfare assistance, 22
caseload numbers on, 1, 13, 15n1
eligibility for, 17n15, 23
methodology used to study, 7, 29n10, 106, 145–152
regression results of study, 107–108, 116n4, 143, 157–164
uniqueness of, xv–xvi, 1–2, 16n3, 23, 29n6, 119
New York City (NYC) welfare study findings, 7–15, 19–29
common elements of work-first programs, 7–9, 8f
(see also Employment retention; Job matching; Job readiness; Partnership)
for-profit providers in, and results, 9–10, 19–20, 21t, 106–108, 107f, 120
full vs. partial performance-based pay to ESP providers in, 10–11, 20, 20t
immediate job search vs. short-term job training in, 11–12, 77–79, 109–111
management practices vs. strategic decisions in, 15, 139–144
nonprofits' mission effectiveness, 121
quick-placement vs. case-management approaches in, 6n13, 13–15, 16n11, 69–77
New York Community Trust, grants from, 93
New York Job Partners (firm), Brooklyn, 21t, 90
New York State, 119
constitutional guarantees in, xv, 1, 22–23, 26–27
sanction rules in, 114, 116
Nonprofit vs. profit organizations as ESP providers, 7, 19–20, 21t, 74, 89–92, 92f, 96f, 101n5, 101nn2–3, 106–108, 107f, 119–126, 127ff
effectiveness of, 121–123
Northern Manhattan Improvement Corp., ESP program of, 21t
NYANA (organization), Brooklyn, ESP program of, 21t
NYC. See New York City (NYC)

One-Stop Career Centers, WIA and, 3–4
Oregon, welfare-to-work programs in, 12

Parents, custodial
as NYC study participants, 150t, 159t, 161t, 162t, 163t, 164t
practice outcomes and, 114, 127ff
as unemployable, 82
Partnership, 144
engagement approach to creating, 39–41, 41n1, 42n3
spirit of, developed by work-first providers, 7–8, 8f, 9, 33–42
usefulness of, 33, 37–38
Performance analysis methodology, 145–152, 151n1
investigation of effective practices in, 147–148, 148f, 151nn5–6
random assignment in, 149–151

Performance analysis methodology, *cont.*
  sample definition in, 146–147
  sample means in, 148–149, 152n7
  site-level practices in, 145–146, 149t, 151nn2–4
  study participant characteristics, 150t
Performance-based contracts
  full vs. partial, to pay ESP providers in NYC, 10–11, 16n9, 93, 101n6, 115–116, 143
  gaming and, 66, 99
  leadership vs. management and, 15, 143–144, 144n1
  pay-for-performance dollars with bonuses in, 20, 20f, 72, 74
  private providers with, for their welfare-to-work services, 1, 58, 59n7, 90
Personal Responsibility and Work Opportunity Reconciliation Act (PRWORA), work-first approach of, 2–3
Personalized assistance, 13, 14, 72
Physical disabilities, services for, 4, 14, 82
Portland, Oregon, JOBS in, 12, 16n11
Poverty rates, 5–6, 6, 16n7
Prison recidivism, addressing, 29n6, 106
Probation approach, creating partnership with, 40
Program performance
  adopting better practices and, 115–116, 143–144, 144n1
  alternative definitions of, as suboptimal practice, 140–141
  broad strategic decision-making and, 15, 139–144
  competency traps as suboptimal for, 141–142
  ESP sites and, 25–28, 26f, 27f, 29nn10–13, 57–58
  frontline management practices and, 15, 129
  gender and, 114–115
  incentives for, 59n7, 92–93, 101n6, 107, 108–109, 114, 116n3, 116n5, 123, 126n1, 140–141
  leadership vs. management and, 15, 143–144, 144n1
  negligible factors in work-first, 112–114
  positive factors in work-first, 106–112, 119
  See also Performance-based contracts
Project Match, Chicago, employee retention at, 61–62
PRWORA (Personal Responsibility and Work Opportunity Reconciliation Act), 2–3
Public assistance, 5, 48
Public policies, 3, 6, 116, 142–143
Public service jobs, 22, 144
  agency contracts for, 115, 123

Queens, NYC
  ESP programs in, 21t, 159t, 161t, 162t, 163t, 164t
  welfare recipients in, 150–151
Quick-placement approach to welfare reform
  case management vs., 13–15, 16n11, 16n13, 59n7, 69–77, 76f, 111–112, 117nn12–13, 142, 151n2
  job-readiness workshops and, 73–74
  program practices within, 72–75
  rationale for, 71–72, 115–116, 143

Reemployment services, 64
  rapid reattachment in, 65–66, 99
Rehabilitation Act (1973), vocational assistance under, 4
Retention specialists, work-first providers as, 9
Riverside, California, GAIN in, 12, 16n11

Safety-net programs, states with, 1, 22–23, 114–115

St. Nicholas Neighborhood Preservation
  Corp., Brooklyn, ESP program of,
  21*t*
San Diego, California, private providers
  of welfare-to-work services in, 1
San Jose, California. Center for
  Employment Training in, 41–42*n*2
Sanctions, 34, 86
  creaming opportunities for, 125,
    126*n*2, 127*f*
  deassignment vs., 87, 88*n*11, 100,
    100*f*, 127*f*
  noncompliance and, 3, 22, 25–26,
    26–27, 85–87, 85*f*, 91–92, 113–
    114, 149*t*
  program performance and, 113–114,
    116
  program size and, 97, 97*f*
  referral to, by EarnFair vs. other
    programs, 94, 94*f*
SAP programs. *See* Skills Assessment
  and Job Placement programs
Screening
  for employment barriers, 84
  job developers and, 53–54, 55
SEEDCO, as prime contractor for CBOs,
  92–96, 101*n*6
Service providers, 17*n*15, 101*n*1
  "Back-to-Work" providers in NYC,
    19, 28*n*2
  faith-based vs. secular organizations
    as, 90, 96*f*, 98–101, 100*f*, 114
  government vs. private, for welfare-
    to-work programs, 1, 19, 98
  nonprofit vs. profit organizations
    as, 7, 19–20, 21*t*, 89–92, 92*f*, 96*f*,
    101*nn*2–3, 106–108, 107*f*, 119–
    126, 127*ff*
  private providers among, 1, 8, 58,
    59*n*7, 78, 90, 119
  program size and, 95–98, 97*f*, 109,
    112–113, 149*t*
  See also Employment Service and
    Placement (ESP) programs; Skills
    Assessment and Job Placement
    (SAP) programs

Skill-building programs, evaluation of, 2
Skills Assessment and Job Placement
  (SAP) programs, NYC and, 19–
  20, 28*n*2
Skills tests, ESP programs and, 24
Smith, Karen, quoted on management
  issues, 44, 58, 59*n*7, 62, 90
Social services, 74, 98, 142
Social workers, quick-placement
  approach and, 72, 73, 84
Staten Island, NYC, ESP programs in,
  21*t*, 159*t*, 161*t*, 162*t*, 163*t*, 164*t*
Stewart, Linda, quoted on management
  issues, 74
Strategic decision-making
  broad, and program performance, 15,
    139–144
  nonprofit vs. profit and, 90, 121–123,
    122*ff*
Substance abuse
  deassignment vs. sanctions for, 87,
    88*n*11
  as significant employment barrier, 14,
    82
Supported Work Demonstration, gender
  differences, 114

TAA (Trade Adjustment Assistance), 3, 4
TANF. *See* Temporary Assistance to
  Needy Families program
Teamwork, NYC welfare staff and
  service providers, 17*n*15
Temporary Assistance to Needy Families
  (TANF) program, xv, 58*n*1, 150*t*
  caseloads on, 1, 3, 15–16*n*2
  funding of, 3, 16*n*5
  meeting new, rules, 6–7, 84
  reauthorization of, 6, 16*n*8
Texas, private providers of welfare-to-
  work services in, 1
Time limits
  education-first welfare reform with, 3
  safety-net programs without, 1, 22–
    23, 26–27

Index   181

Trade Adjustment Assistance (TAA), state implementation and federal funding of, 3, 4
Tradeoffs, welfare vs. periods of work, 45
Training programs, 3, 8, 41–42n2
  certificates upon completion of, 24, 36
  education and, 4, 11–12, 16n10
  employment and, assistance, 4, 81
  referrals to, 159t, 161t, 162t, 163t, 164t
  short-term, for jobs (see Job-training programs)
Training vouchers
  eligibility for, 80, 101n4
  HRA and, 16n10, 24–25, 29n8
  percentage participants who receive, 78, 78f, 92, 92f, 94f, 97–98, 97f
Transportation issues, overcoming, 13, 25
Trust-building
  program size and, 96–97
  spirit of partnership and, 8, 33, 34, 36–37, 41n1

Unemployed veterans, employment and training assistance for, 4
Unemployment, 44, 82
  inconsistent work patterns and, 5–6
  lack of jobs to hold and, 29n12
  rapid reattachment in case of, 65–66

VendorStat, as welfare-to-work accountability tool, 21–22, 28–29n5, 28n4, 93
Veterans services, state implementation and federal funding of, 3, 4
Vocational education, TANF-funded training in, 3
Vocational issues, quick-placement approach and, 73
Vocational rehabilitation, state implementation and federal funding of, 3

Wages, 6
  career advancement and, 95–96
  minimum wage, 5, 16n6, 77
Wages, high
  definition of, 57, 59n5, 106
  ESP performance payment and, 20, 20f
Welfare caseloads, 20
  closed, and ESP performance payment, 20, 20f
  factors contributing to reduction of, xv, 6, 16n6, 16n8
  number of, in NYC, xv, 1, 13, 15n1, 15–16n2, 96
  number of, in U.S., 3, 150t
Welfare policies, as work-oriented in U.S., 6
Welfare reform, 5
  education-first vs. work-first in, xviii, 2–3
  federal legislation for, xv, 2, 42n1
  strategies in, xvii–xix, 15, 139–144
Welfare reform approaches
  education-first, 3, 12, 16n12
  mixed initial activities, 11–12, 16n11
  quick-placement vs. case-management, 13–15, 16n11, 16n13, 69–77, 111–112, 151n2
  work-first, 2–3
  (see also entries beginning Work-first . . .)
Welfare-to-work improvements needed, 4–15
  addressing poverty rates among program leavers, 5–6
  adopting better practices, 105, 115–116, 144
  avoiding use of suboptimal practices, 143–144, 144n1
  meeting new TANF rules, 6–7
  study findings in NYC on (see New York City [NYC] welfare study findings)

Welfare-to-work program management,
    xvii–xviii, 44, 56–57, 58, 59n7,
    89–91, 98–99, 110
  caseload employment rates by NYC
    site, 133f, 138f
  effective strategies in, 137–138, 139
  frontline practices vs. service
    strategies in, 134–138, 138f
  literature on, 129–131
  NYC sites and, 131–134
  quotes by, 52, 62, 71, 72, 74, 79, 81,
    89, 90, 91
  suboptimal work-first practices in,
    139–143
Welfare-to-work programs, xv, 113
  different practices among NYC,
    69–88, 119
  evaluation of, xviii–xix, 21–22,
    28n4, 28–29n5
  government vs. private service
    providers for, 1, 19, 98
  management of (*see* Welfare-to-work
    program management; Work-first
    welfare reform)
  random assignments to, in NYC, 2,
    11, 16n4, 105, 149–151
  staffing of, 33, 34–35, 41, 42n3, 46,
    50n1, 50nn3–4, 55, 96
  types of NYC, 89–102
    See also specifics, e.g., Greater
    Avenues for Independence
    (GAIN); Supported Work
    Demonstration
WEP (Work Experience Program), NYC,
  22, 25
WHEDCo (organization), Bronx, ESP
  program of, 21t
White non-Hispanic persons, as NYC vs.
  U.S. TANF participants, 150t
WIA (Workforce Investment Act), 3–4,
  58n1
Wildcat Industries, management of, 44,
  58, 59n7, 62
Wildcat Service Corporation, ESP
  program of, 20, 21t, 44

Wisconsin, private service providers in,
  1, 19
Women, 82, 114, 117n15
  employee retention of, as custodial
    persons, 10, 106
  See also Mothers
Work Experience Program (WEP), as
  NYC version of public service
  jobs, 22, 25
Work-first factors of negligible
  consequence, 112–114
  deassignment, 112
  faith-based programs, 114
  program size, 109, 112–113
  sanctioning rates, 113–114
Work-first factors of positive
  consequence, 106–112
  for-profit providers, 106–108, 107f,
    116nn1–2, 119, 159t, 161t, 162t,
    163t, 164t
  immediate job search, 109–111
  performance incentives, 108–109,
    140–141
  quick-placement approach, 111–112
Work-first welfare reform, xviii, 2
  common elements used by providers
    of, 7–9, 8f
  differences among NYC welfare-to-
    work programs, 69–88
  effectiveness of, 105–106, 115–116,
    121–123, 137–138, 138f
    (*see also* Work-first factors of
    negligible consequence; Work-first
    factors of positive consequence)
Workfare programs. *See* Work
  Experience Program (WEP), NYC
Workforce Investment Act (WIA), 3–4,
  58n1

About the Institute

The W.E. Upjohn Institute for Employment Research is a nonprofit research organization devoted to finding and promoting solutions to employment-related problems at the national, state, and local levels. It is an activity of the W.E. Upjohn Unemployment Trustee Corporation, which was established in 1932 to administer a fund set aside by Dr. W.E. Upjohn, founder of The Upjohn Company, to seek ways to counteract the loss of employment income during economic downturns.

The Institute is funded largely by income from the W.E. Upjohn Unemployment Trust, supplemented by outside grants, contracts, and sales of publications. Activities of the Institute comprise the following elements: 1) a research program conducted by a resident staff of professional social scientists; 2) a competitive grant program, which expands and complements the internal research program by providing financial support to researchers outside the Institute; 3) a publications program, which provides the major vehicle for disseminating the research of staff and grantees, as well as other selected works in the field; and 4) an Employment Management Services division, which manages most of the publicly funded employment and training programs in the local area.

The broad objectives of the Institute's research, grant, and publication programs are to 1) promote scholarship and experimentation on issues of public and private employment and unemployment policy, and 2) make knowledge and scholarship relevant and useful to policymakers in their pursuit of solutions to employment and unemployment problems.

Current areas of concentration for these programs include causes, consequences, and measures to alleviate unemployment; social insurance and income maintenance programs; compensation; workforce quality; work arrangements; family labor issues; labor-management relations; and regional economic development and local labor markets.